PRAISE FOR R[illegible]RAIN

“An enga[illegible] heart beating at i[illegible]

“Raw. Riveting[illegible]ain stays true to its title as it explores th[illegible] pain of a teenager desperately trying to find peace in a world full of pain. Lee Matthew Goldberg is a master at bestowing sympathy and strength on deeply flawed characters. Realistic and shocking, hopeful and satisfying, Runaway Train will keep readers turning the page.” —*USA Today* Bestselling Author Rebecca Forster

“It’s an incredibly challenging task for an author to utilize a darkly comedic tone without coming across as disingenuous—but Goldberg executes it here with expert precision. Brimming over with the visceral atmosphere of the early 90s grunge era, RUNAWAY TRAIN is a must-read for those willing to buckle up for the ride.” —Peter Malone Elliott (Director of Operations, Book Pipeline)

“In *Runaway Train*, Nico takes the leap every teenager dreams of taking, but it’s a leap few writers have handled as well as Goldberg. He pulls apart the teen puzzle of feeling both adrift and intentional in the same moment and reminds us that finding a way to be heard is the only way anybody finds themselves.” —Rick Polito, forthcoming author of *Off Trail*

RUNAWAY TRAIN

RUNAWAY TRAIN

• • • • • • •

LEE MATTHEW GOLDBERG

WISE WOLF BOOKS LAS VEGAS

WISE WOLF
BOOKS

This is a work of fiction. All of the characters, organizations, publications, and events portrayed in this novel are either products of the author's imagination or are used fictitiously.

For information, address Wolfpack Publishing,
5130 S. Fort Apache Road, 215-380 Las Vegas, NV 89148

wisewolfbooks.com

Cover design by Wise Wolf Books

Paperback ISBN 978-1-953944-03-0
eBook ISBN 978-1-953944-01-6
LOCN 2020952524

First Edition: April 2021

FOR DAD, WHO LOVED TO READ

Bought a ticket for a runaway train
Like a madman laughing at the rain
Little out of touch, little insane
It's just easier than dealing with the pain

Runaway train, never goin' back
Wrong way on a one-way track
Seems like I should be getting somewhere
Somehow I'm neither here nor there
-Soul Asylum "Runaway Train"

SIDE A

• • • • •

March 1994

1

• • • • •

Dead & Bloated – Stone Temple Pilots

My sister Kristen died the same day as the actor River Phoenix, October 31st, 1993, he from a drug overdose in the middle of the night outside the Viper Room, her on an early morning run through Laurel Canyon, two days before her seventeenth birthday—and a happy fucking Halloween to me. There I was, dressed up in costume as D'arcy, the bassist from Smashing Pumpkins: oversized baggy striped sweater, dyed blond hair, a dab of red lips and blue eye shadow, and a broken bass guitar slung around my shoulder that I didn't know how to play anyway, watching the news where I saw River's lean body, which I had imagined climbing on top of me multiple times, being hauled away on a stretcher, when the doorbell rang and a police officer asked if my parents were home.

"Er...no," I said, running through my mind the millions of bad things I may have done. That strappy dress I'd shoplifted, the bag of dirt I sold to a freshman pretending it was weed.

"Are you a relative of Kristen Sullivan?"

Kristen? What could the police want with perfect Kristen?

"Yeah. Her sister."

"I am sorry to tell you this, but your sister has died."

I truly believed that if I slammed the door on the cop, what they said wouldn't be real. That's how mental I was. A montage of River Phoenix appeared on the television. Stand By Me, Running on Empty, A Night in the Life of Jimmy Reardon, and as the gay hustler in My Own Private Idaho, where I truly fell in love. I didn't know if I was crying for him or Kristen, all I knew was that after rubbing my eyes, my hands were blackened from the mascara stains.

The police officer went on to tell me what happened. Kristen was going for a run when she collapsed. A neighbor called the paramedics, but she was DOA likely from a brain aneurysm, the same thing that took my grandfather when he was super young too.

My own brain felt weighted, as if both their afflictions had insidiously traveled down the street and filtered into my cranium. Kristen and I were so close in age, Irish twins just eleven months apart, and the horror of thinking this might happen to me next became too much to deal.

"Where are your parents?" the police officer asked, sober and to the point, bringing me back from the brink of insanity. "Is there a number we can reach them at?"

Dad was surely at work, specializing in finance litigation, whatever the hell that meant, usually into the office by 7:00 a.m. and home sometimes around midnight, a ghost who occasionally graced us with his presence. Mom was a secretary in an ad agency, and possibly still home. I heard a voice calling down from up above asking who it was. Mom's face emerged at the top of the stairs. She had a hair crimper still smoking in her hand and wore a blouse with thick shoulder pads. Her nose twitched and then she sneezed. I couldn't watch her heart break too so I just ran upstairs.

Instead of my room, I bolted into Kristen's who kept it immaculate. Posters of Jason Priestly from 90210 adorned the walls. I was more of a Luke Perry gal with his bad-boy sideburns and scowl, and a receding hairline that I longed to stroke as he'd nestle his angular head into my lap so I could stare into his brooding eyes.

I flopped on Kristen's bed, smelling the Sunflowers perfume still clinging to her pillow, and stared around her room. Sports trophies galore: track and field and volleyball, even basketball, which was her secondary sport. An Ace of Base poster taped to the ceiling. She would blast "The Sign," and I'd reply by turning up Soundgarden or Nirvana or Pearl Jam or Smashing Pumpkins or Mother Love Bone, or any kind of real music to drown out the shitty pop shit she loved so much. That was Kristen, a pop song: silky blond hair, hella popular at school but never a mean girl. She had so many friends I could never keep track of them all while I just had two: Winter and Jeremy, our super-exclusive trio of burnouts, terrible grades, and contempt for everyone else who pretended like they were in a 90210 episode. If I'd ever be prevented from graduating, no one would chant "Nico Sullivan Graduates" as they did for frog-faced Donna Martin.

Yes, my name is Nico, short for Nicole but no one

has called me that since I was a little kid. Too pedestrian. Nico smokes long cigarettes while Nicole liked ponies. Nico uses her fake ID to get into clubs and listen to hella angry music where sweaty dudes with long hair in flannel shirts rage about the government and our lame parents and the War on Drugs and the AIDS crisis and old George Bush who'd finally been replaced by saxophone playing cool guy Bill Clinton—who I'd totally do—and then the two of us would share like five post-coital Big Macs because I know he'd be into that.

Kristen's dead.

The thought stayed trapped between my ears. It had floated away momentarily only to come racing back with venom. My beautiful sister who I barely spent any time with, who I honestly resented because she didn't have a muffin top body like mine and pasty skin and a smile that showed too much of her upper gums. I pictured her lying lonely on the ground when the aneurysm struck. Could she tell what was going on? Did she see the light as it took her away? Was she thinking of me?

God, how narcissistic I could be.

I whipped out a cigarette and lit it out the window, puffed away and contemplated leaping outside, two dead daughters in one horror of a day for my folks. I knew they'd mourn Kristen more. I was an afterthought, an oh right Nico's there too, more of a ghost in the house than even my dad. I spent as much time away from home as possible, escaping with Winter and Jeremy.

I carefully listened at the door to hear if the cop was still there. I heard Mom weeping, dark sounds coming up from deep within her soul. I put out my cigarette and rushed out of Kristen's room. Grabbing my Walkman, I booked it out of the house before anyone could stop me, not wanting to deal with Mom trying to comfort me or vice-versa. Headphones on, listening to my Stone Temple Pilots tape as the song "Dead & Bloated" shattered my eardrums. I turned up the volume to the max as the song took over the world.

I hit rewind and played the song over and over, singing it at the top of my lungs, causing our neighbor Mr. Ferguson to waddle outside in his backyard and give me the side-eye because of our low fences. But then I could hear the police cruiser wailing as it drove away, and I was forced to confront my sad, sad reality again.

• • •

Almost six months after Kristen's death, and Winter, Jeremy and I have gotten in the habit of skipping school on the last day of every month to head to the Viper Room and mourn River Phoenix's passing, even though I'm honestly mourning Kristen's. This is how our day of hooky begins. Jeremy brings a bottle of vodka, Winter supplies the weed, and I'm responsible for cigs. We get on the train to Sunset Boulevard in West Hollywood and carry peonies and leave them outside with all the other accouterments adoring fans had bestowed. By the time we get there, we're all shit-faced and stumbling: Winter's eyes spinning, Jeremy letting go of his masculinity and sashaying down the street like a runway model. Then we all hug and cry and quote from Stand By Me.

"Yeah, but so what? Everybody's weird," we scream at the sky. "Weird, weird, weird!"

Winter, Jeremy and I certainly like to think of ourselves as the weirdest of the weird. Winter with her dyed Manic Panic white hair and giant boobs, her Jansport backpack with pot leaves sewn on and liquor bottles clinking inside, her choker necklace practically cutting off her circulation, her rusty Doc Martins with the yellow laces untied, dark lip liner with really light lip gloss and a leotard with a snap crotch. And Jeremy, sweet Cupid-faced Jeremy with rosy cheeks looking like he's still a freshman, super baggy jeans to hide his chicken legs, hair parted right down the middle with bangs curling over his eyes, the tips frosted blond. I lost my virginity to Jeremy when we were fourteen, sleeping over at his house, his mom without a clue, drunk on cough syrup with Tori Amos' Little Earthquakes getting us in the mood (I should've known he was gay then). I, of course, made the first move because Winter had done it a ton of times already and I was tired of her holding it over me. But Jeremy kept slipping out like a fish trying to escape back into water. He felt me up a little, even tried to go down on me, but he looked like he was trying to figure out the answers to a Chemistry quiz.

"Jeremy, are you gay?" I asked, pushing his diligent face away from my crotch. Jeremy had a poster of Luke Perry from 90210 too, and Luke Perry gave us a look that said, duh, the kid jerks off to me every night.

"It's okay if you are. Like, I have a cousin who is and lives in Palm Springs. He has a Chihuahua and a boyfriend named Kipper. Winter and I still love you."

Jeremy didn't respond, just cried. I didn't know what to do so I held him as "Silent All These Years" played and my heart broke that he had to keep this bottled up inside for so long. I made a vow to break anyone's arm that might mess with him.

Winter, Jeremy, and I formed our clique as protection. Kristen went to a private school because she had the grades for it, but my delinquent ass had no other choice but the public shitbox in Reseda. Jocks and pretty girls do okay at the school, theater kids even have a home, and the rest of us blend into obscurity. Winter, Jeremy and I decided not to let anyone else in (except for hella cute dudes to occasionally mess around with at parties we'd crash, at least for Winter and me), and no one else bothers us. We roam the halls, arm-in-arm, most people thinking Winter and I are lez (I mean, we made out a few times but BFD—Big. Fuckin. Deal).

Now we wander away from the Viper Room, Jeremy doing his impression of Gordie from Stand By Me when he gets the leech stuck to his dick, and then we meander into a back alley where we can get good and sloppy.

Winter yanks a fresh vodka bottle from her Jansport, twists off the cap, and chugs before passing it my way. The liquor burns like a match down my throat.

"God, River Phoenix was twenty-three!" Winter moans. "Can you imagine dying in like six or seven years?"

Can you imagine dying in just a few months like my sister did when she hit seventeen? I want to say, but I really never talk about Kristen. Winter and Jeremy are always either too caught up in their own bullshit to ask, or wisely know it would only sour the day.

"Who would you be, like, the most sad if they died?" Jeremy asks. "Famous person-wise."

"Kurt Cobain!" I screech, because the walls in my bedroom held evidence of my absolute and devoted love for him. Screw Courtney Love who gets to sleep with him every day on their bed of lovely unwashed sheets. I long to comb his dirty hair, sniff his moth-eaten sweaters, bleed across his book of poetry, birth his child, have him call me Mom, write a song for me to sing at one of his shows, and then Courtney Love and I could have a cat flight backstage because I took her man and would never give him back.

Winter and Jeremy agree with my choice, but Jeremy says: "Chris Cornell would make me cry. I mean, Kurt Cobain is the better songwriter, but I'd give up my cherry for Chris Cornell."

"You already gave up your cherry to Nico," Winter adds, always the smart ass.

"Any fish I ever had doesn't count," Jeremy says, fluttering his eyes. "No offense, Nico."

"None taken. I turned you gay. I can live with that."

Winter takes another swig that she chases with a hit of pot from her swirly glass pipe. It isn't even eleven in the morning, and like, a Tuesday, but the three of us are on the road to getting more messed up than ever before. I love it with every fiber of my being.

"Mine would be Eddie Vedder," Winter says, coughing like crazy. "He just oozes sex appeal. Like a god."

And then she begins singing "Jeremy" to Jeremy, which is something the two of us do from time to time because it pisses him off so.

"What dead person would you want back the most?" Jeremy asks, sticking his tongue in Winter's heavily-pierced ear to annoy her.

"Joplin," Winter says, smacking him on the cheek. "Because my mom would go ape-shit. She loves Janis Joplin so much. She always talks about Woodstock and how ah-may-zing it was."

"Mine would really be Freddie Mercury," Jeremy says. "Because he was such a gay icon. Like, AIDS is the WORST."

We toast to AIDS being the WORST and briefly mention a kid at our school that had to leave when he contracted HIV.

"Nico, who would you bring back?" Winter asks. She takes my hand. Hers is clammy, but mine is worse. Does she want me to say my sister? Since I never talk about Kristen, maybe this is Winter's way of getting me to release some of my demons. Brilliant and cunning Winter.

"River Phoenix, of course!" I shout, choking on tears that feel like a hard-shelled walnut struggling down my gullet. Winter and Jeremy both look at me, disappointed, their eyes saying it's time to talk about Kristen and how much her passing affects me.

"It's okay, love," Jeremy says, caressing my cheek like one would to a cat. "We're here for you."

I try to speak, but only a sad bubble emerges from my lips before it pops. I turn to Winter and lunge.

"Gimme some of that pot."

We wrestle around on the dirty pavement, me tickling Winter's ribs, her laughing and sounding like a squeaking mouse. I wrap my thick thighs around her and she honks my boob, then she reaches in her pocket and puts a baggie between her teeth.

"Kiss me and take it," she says, as we hear the sound of a police siren. My heart shatters in two, not because of our truancy but because the sound of the police always brings me right back to that fucking awful Halloween day.

I jump off of her, hug myself, and motor out of the alleyway. A homeless crackhead is being arrested. He's trying to bite his shoulder as the cops attempt to put him in handcuffs. He's hollering at the sun, and through my own drug-fueled haze I see myself in his place: fighting against my assailants in blue, raging from a cocktail of uppers and downers, a true mess being put out of her misery for good. Dead & Bloated. Zipped up in a body bag and taken to a cold freezer, just like Kristen, so we could be put in the ground together, her spirit playing Ace of Base while mine blasted STP, a warring duel of specters fighting to be the loudest one in heaven. Or honestly, she'd be the one up there doing the Running Man with God to "The Sign," while I'd be sent farther down below to spend an eternity in a mosh pit with Satan and all the other absolute trainwrecks, getting licked by the flames.

2

Sex Type Thing – Stone Temple Pilots

Forget what anyone tells you about the bus in L.A. Even though I'd been given Kristen's old car and got my license at sixteen, a car is no bueno when you're high as the sky; but the bus has oodles of various souls from all over the city mashed together on a highway moving a mile every ten minutes. I love the feel of all these strangers forced to associate with one another, something that barely exists due to L.A.'s isolated car culture. We travel in boxes here, shut-in and refusing to connect; I'm the poster child for this anti-social behavior. And since I'd never risk getting a DUI and losing my teal blue Hyundai Excel—my lifeline, my means of escape if ever need be—the bus becomes my primary transport when inebriated. So I leave Winter and Jeremy flailing around in the alleyway by the Viper Room because I'm jonesing for a sandwich, have nil cash with me, and want to go home and blast some STP Core with the new CD I'd pilfered from the local Sam Goody.

Reaching home in the middle of a Tuesday when I should've been at school, Laurel Canyon has an eerie quality of a Sci-Fi tale where a UFO zapped up all its suburban citizens. Not that the neighborhood is a pillar of action normally, but during the week it's deader than dead, dead, dead. I check my eyes in my compact mirror to make sure they aren't mega bloodshot, then take a sniff of my Alice and Chains T-shirt in case it smelled of pot. I realize I'm being stupid, since the 'rents are both at work. Honestly, they'd even be clueless if they caught me swimming in a pool filled with vodka.

When I step inside, electricity tinges in the air, the sensation of a television being left on. I make my way into the kitchen and throw together a salami and American cheese sandwich, heavy on the mayo. I shovel the sandwich into my mouth, practically forgetting how to chew as I kick off my Doc Martins and leap up the stairs like I'm a kid playing hopscotch. Walking down the hallway, I keep my eyes away from Kristen's room immortalized by my folks, the door firmly shut. The last time I'd been inside was the Halloween day Kristen had died. I never summoned up enough courage to re-enter.

A squeaking sound echoed down the hallway. At first, I think it's a mouse, but the squeaking gets louder, followed by moans and a cringe-inducing oh God, oh God, oh Goddddddddddddd that couldn't belong to anyone but my mother who had the low bass voice of a sportscaster. Do my parents seriously meet up for lunchtime quickies when they figure I wouldn't be around? The thought makes me want to gag on my salami. I immediately want to tell Kristen; we only bonded in making fun of the 'rents, but I quickly eject that solemn idea.

It makes zero sense that my parents could be copulating, since they barely say boo to one another. Since Kristen's passing, my dad spends even more time at work, sometimes sleeping on a cot in his office. We'd been to family therapy a bunch where Mom and Dad argued about how much they reminded each other of Kristen, since she's a combination of both their features: Mom's long, snooty nose and luscious hair, Dad's wide-set eyes and strong chin. Hello, I want to say, what about me? I'm still here and if you two would get your heads out of your asses for one freaking second, you'd realize that I just lost someone too!

So, it couldn't be Mom and Dad bumping uglies, which leads me to imagine Mom alone with a vibrating friend, too disgusting to even picture for one second.

I start to back away when I hear, "Luanne, Luanne, Luanne," from a voice that's Definitely. Not. My. Father's!

"Oh Roggggggger," my mom shrieks, reaching a climax as she cooes the barfy name of our sad sack, duck-footed, pot-bellied, comb-over neighbor Roger Ferguson who always has food stuck in his teeth and would ask me to pull his finger at backyard grill-outs. Ferguson's divorced, has two little shits that only live with him on the weekends, and a giant chow chow named Shirley who resembles him and takes dumps the size of small logs on our front lawn.

Had I not been high, I might've kept backing out of the house and not confronted the filthy act happening a few steps away, but instead I march into my room, throw STP's Core into my stereo system and crank up

"Sex Type Thing" loud enough to shake the walls. Screams follow from my mother's room and then I meet the two gross lovebirds outside in the hallway: Roger Ferguson trying to cover up his unmentionables with a floral blanket and failing, and my mother in my dad's goddamn bathrobe, the picture-perfect image of a true homewrecker.

"Nico!" she screeches. "What are you doing home?"

"Oh no," I snap back. "I am not the one in trouble here. What are you doing home, you jezebel?"

She slaps me across the cheek, the sting a throbbing reminder of her infidelity. We stare at each other in shock, both amazed at how cruel we could be. Ferguson slips around us, clearly wanting no part of our tête-à-tête.

"And with Mr. Ferguson!" I yell, loud enough so he could still hear, as he huffs and puffs down the hallway. "He looks like the Stay Puft Marshmallow Man minus the ascot."

"Turn down that music, Nico, those awful, awful sounds."

I follow her into my room where she jabs at the stereo buttons to no avail. Finally, she lifts the system from the table and launches it at the floor.

"What the hell, Mom?" A crack develops down the center as the music murmurs to a sad finish. "That's like five hundred dollars, you crackhead."

She tries to slap me again but I block it, clearly stronger. Mom's kinda skinny with tiny baby wrists.

"I will not have you talking to me that way," she says. She's crying now, her face the color of a red pepper.

"Does Dad know?"

She pulls at her graying hair that she'd given up dyeing after Kristen's death. She chomps her teeth that she'd been grinding. Her eyes are red, her face washed out and lifeless. I should hug her right there. I should've hugged her months ago when Kristen died, but I don't want to be comforted by her, or by Dad, or by anyone.

I've wanted so much space that I created a fortress.

At least to her credit, she respects that.

"Nico," she says, quietly. "You don't understand. I..."

Her body begins heaving like the scene in Alien when the alien bursts from the guy's body. She sits on the edge of my bed and closes Dad's bathrobe to her neck.

"Your father and I haven't been doing well, as I'm sure you know."

"That doesn't mean you should spread your legs to the closest neighbor!"

She cuts me with her eyes, too exhausted to silence my foul mouth. But I enjoy being deplorable. The more terrible I act, the less chance anyone else might try to console me.

She cries more, fat gobs that plop on her thighs. "Nico, I..."

"Save it," I say, charging out of the room. I don't want to deal with her. I need Winter and Jeremy, the only people in my life that don't make me want to smash my fist into the wall.

I could hear her calling out my name, desperate for reconciliation, but I wouldn't give her the satisfaction. Dad may have been a ghost, but he's her ghost, and he never hid his desire for financial success. He pays for our Laurel Canyon four-bedroom, and for their BMW, and gives Mom anything she wants to justify his absence. He's cold and distant, but he's never been any different. She thought she could change him, but guess what lady? Men don't change. I'm just sixteen-and-a-half and I can already tell her that. Jeremy is gay and no contact with my vagina was ever gonna change things. Dad is aloof and will be until the day he dropped. That didn't mean that you can go and screw around on him with the first penis that bounces your way.

I don't have time to wait for the bus and Winter's house is only a mile or so away so I get in Kristen's car and drive, high and mighty, breaking all speed limits, practically begging for a cop to pull me over and put me out of my fucking misery.

• • •

Winter lives at the end of a cul-de-sac in a small house that she and her hippie mom Edina share. Edina is British with orange hair like a pom-pom, usually dressed in a chic muumuu with statement jewelry dangling from her neck and wrists and a thin joint permanently clamped between her lips. By now it's after three and legit for Winter and Jeremy to be home, although Edina could care less if Winter skips school. Sometimes they'd take mother-daughter days and drive to Joshua Tree to get stoned in the sun. Winter's dad had peaced out when she was young, and Edina was always dating some crunchy, Birkenstock-wearing, grey-haired, patchouli-scented dude who would talk about how great the sixties were and how sexily Edina carries herself.

Sure enough, a wafting of pot greets me as Edina opens the door and embraces me with a kiss on both my cheeks.

"This bone structure," she says, examining my face like it's art. "What I'd do for cheeks sharp enough to cut an apple."

Edina says weird phrases like that, but because of her posh Brit accent, they tend to sound profound.

"Baby doll, you've been crying."

"I hate my mother," I say, wrenching out of her grasp.

"Don't we all?" Edina says, with a puff. "Mine was a bitch and half. Caught me once with a boy in my room and called me the town whore."

"You and my mom would have a lot in common then."

Edina scrunches up her face, but she's likely too high to realize what I'd meant.

"You look like you can use a drag," she says, placing the joint between my lips and encouraging me to suck. "Marijuana cures all ailments. Just ask my migraines."

"Is Winter home?"

"Yes, and I have a feeling you girls didn't go to school today." She places a finger over her lips. "Our secret."

"Thanks, Ed."

"Anytime, Nic."

She waves me inside. Winter's house is forever cluttered but homey, unlike my Dad's minimalist design. Tchotchkes galore from Edina's far-flung travels. African busts mix with Gaelic bowls filled with lemons and Asian paintings of naked people bathing. Joan Baez softly sings from out of a record player. Edina sways in delight.

"That voice," Edina says. "I'd drown a drifter to have Joan Baez's voice. Yours is so beautiful too." She pets my hair, and I'm embarrassed because it's probably oily due to not washing it since the weekend. Edina doesn't comment on wanting my hair, she's not one for lies. "You used to sing sometimes in Winter's room. I'd hear it and think, wow, that girl's got something bloody special all right."

"I really need to talk to Winter," I say, not so into listening to any accolades about my voice. I know I have a talent, but my vocal cords for the most part stay silent. I hate singing in front of others, too shy I guess, forever afraid I wouldn't hit the right notes and I'd be brutally mocked. And yeah, I long to sing in a band like any other alterna-chick. Like my dream is to be a female version of Cobain, Weiland, Pirner, or any one of my heroes, but in this life I've decided to remain mute, my voice primarily for the shower, never a crowd.

"All right, darling," Edina says, and dances me toward Winter's room.

The song "Elderly Woman Behind the Counter in a Small Town" by Pearl Jam pours from out of the doorjamb. Inside Jeremy is braiding Winter's Casper-white hair, a menthol cigarette bobbing between his teeth.

"There's our hot little piece," Jeremy says, like some old-timey radio announcer.

"Nico, Jer will braid you next. He learned how to do cornrows."

"I'm thinking of going Barbizon in New York," Jeremy says. "And then becoming a beauty school dropout like Frenchie."

I hate Grease, but know that Jeremy loves it and worships John Travolta on the same level I lurrrrv Cobain.

"My mother's the town Jezebel," I say, flopping onto Winter's bed and playing with her flannel sleeve.

Winter's room is like my own except Eddie Vedder rules the walls with a shrine-like dominance. I fully expect him to put out a restraining order on her one day. A large Vs. poster monopolizes her ceiling, its angora goat's nose trying to wiggle through the barbed-wire fencing. The wall with her lone window is devoted to the movie Singles.

"Luanne the Jezebel?" Jeremy snorts. "Girl, no way. Your mom is firmly in the throes of menopause."

"I caught her and our neighbor Mr. Ferguson humping their brains out."

Jeremy stops braiding. He and Winter's mouths gape open.

"Mr. Ferguson?" Winter says, clapping her hands.

"Bitch, it isn't funny," I yell, yanking at her flannel. She covers her laugh with a half-hearted apology.

"Look, your parents probably haven't touched in a thousand years," Jeremy says. "They are headed for a di-vorce."

"No, they aren't."

"Nico, I saw it with mine. When they're not fighting, they aren't speaking, right? They'll be happier apart."

I think about which one I'd want to live with, deciding on neither: Mom too pathetic, Dad too sterile and glum.

"Double the gifts on Christmas," Jeremy says, holding out his hand for a high-five. I leave him hanging.

"Neither gives a shit about me," I say. "Like, even when Kristen was alive."

I see Winter and Jeremy eyeing each other carefully, both of them alarmed that I mentioned Kristen's name.

"Like, Kristen was the easy daughter who brought home top grades and sports trophies. They barely had to parent. And then there's me. I require like four parents to monitor my delinquent ass."

"They love you," Jeremy says. "They just don't know how to show it."

"I want to run away," I mumble, to the Eddie Vedder poster hanging on the wall.

Winter pops up. "Girl, you should!"

She's probably still wired from the alcohol/pot we ingested earlier.

"We all should!" Winter yelps, smiling her wicked smile and then hugging me tight so our cheeks mushed together. "Like, forget school this semester, right?" she adds. "We're all pretty much flunking anyway. We should go to Seattle where like the grunge scene is really happening. I want to go to dirty dive bars and make out with boys who have hair covering their eyes."

"You do that here," I say.

"Yeah, but L.A. is so whack. Like, all the grunge kids here are so fake. They love Nirvana because Nirvana is popular, but I want to interact with people who love grunge because they need it in their soul to survive. Like I do."

"You just want to screw Eddie Vedder," I say.

"And you want to screw Kurt Cobain, Jer wants

to screw all of Soundgarden. So what? We'll whore it up and down Seattle and leave just when the pitchforks come out."

"You're not serious."

Winter pushes a lock of hair behind my ear and kisses me on the cheek. Her eyes are so glassy, like looking into a pool. "Nico, you are really sad. I can feel it."

"I just caught my mom–"

She whips her head back and forth. "No, like, you never talk about your sister, but it's okay, we're here to listen. And then we want you have fun and get all that melancholy outta your system."

Hearing Winter talk about Kristen makes my insides rumble and slap into one another. Maybe I do need to talk about her more, but it's just so damn hard. Especially because deep down I fear that Kristen's fate would soon become my own. I'm pretty sure my grandfather died from the same goddamn thing at a young goddamn age, so what kind of chance do I possibly have to escape that wicked destiny?

"Isn't there like a million things you want to do?" Winter asks.

Secretly, she's completely right. After Kristen died, I'd made a bucket list I carry around at the bottom of my backpack. Sometimes I take it out and pour over its wild contents that ranged from surfing, to climbing a mountain and facing my fear of heights, to kissing a boy I really had feelings for, to getting up in front of an audience and singing my heart out, and even visiting Kurt Cobain's house and having the courage to knock on the door, push stupid Courtney Love aside, and tell him how much his words mean to invisible me.

"I wrote down a bucket list," I say.

Winter squeals, something she does often that annoys me. I cover my ears.

"Yes bitch, yes! You have to do every item on that bucket list. Like, Jer and I will help you do them. We'll take your car and go on a road trip."

"What about school?"

"My mom will cover for us. She's done it for me before and it's always fine. Like, our school is so dumb and big they don't care who shows up. You'll tell your parents you're staying at my house for a while and then just call home every few days so they don't get suspicious. It's foolproof."

She jumps off her bed, rummages through a drawer, and pulls out a baggie of weed. She packs her swirly glass pipe and inhales. I know that's what's causing her neurons to fire so dramatically, but I can't deny that the idea excites me to no end. Winter then takes out her Pearl Jam CD and puts on STP's Core.

"I know you're big into STP right now and Scott Weiland's wang." She smiles and cues up "Sex Type Thing," singing loud enough to make her throat sore. "We're gonna find you a boy, Nico, when we run away, a yummy, grungy boy who plays guitar like the devil and screws like no L.A. jerkoff could."

I imagine this boy: Cobain-esque with a thin body, multi-colored hair, and a sweater too big for his frame, big enough for me to fit inside of it as well. He'd take me back to his room, turn on his black light, play me some delicious Nirvana on his guitar and then kiss me hard, refusing to let go of my tongue. And he'd taste like Zima because that's what we'd drink until we reached oblivion.

"Runaway." I giggle as Winter passes me the pipe. "Like, that would show my parents."

"It's not about your whack parents, it's about you, Nico. Being free. Becoming a woman."

I take a hit, letting it tickle my senses. Jeremy squeals even louder than Winter and says he's in too.

"I love you both," I say, and Winter kisses me on the lips, tasting of the cherry ring pop on her finger.

"I love you more, lovely," Winter says. She starts dancing, flinging her arms without abandon.

Jeremy dances with her, jumping around like a fool. They both beckon me to join. I think of Kristen, who'd shake her head at us being so ridiculous, but maybe she'd be happy I decided to run away like this. From up above, she couldn't be pleased that I'm so miserable. She'd want me to live again, whatever it takes to get there. So I dance like no one is watching, like I'd entered my own universe while I imagine all the travels I'll embark on, this runaway child is ready.

After about an hour of jumping around, the three of us collapse into a ball of sweaty laughter as the CD ends with "Where the River Goes."

"Will you tell me what the rent's like in heaven, Kristen?" I whisper, my mouth feeling full of cotton. "Will you stop doing the Running Man with God for long enough to tell me you're okay? I miss you. I love you. I never gave you the mixtape I made for your seventeenth birthday. I hate that you might've thought I didn't care. Because I always really did."

I get up and lurch out of Winter's house toward my car with a million fallen tears left in my path.

3

• • • • •

Runaway Train – Soul Asylum

The grunge mixtape I'd made for Kristen has become a permanent fixture in my life, rotating from the car's tape deck to my Sony Sports Walkman as if it possesses the uncanny ability to keep me further connected to her. We'd gotten into a fight before she died. Not a knockdown, drag-out, hair-pulling kind of battle—more so a test of willpower. I'd taken to smoking cigarettes in my room. This was a new phase. Before I'd previously sneak them in the backyard, but my personality was starting to veer toward not giving a flying pig. She complained about the dangers of secondhand smoke and that she could smell it in her room. I told her she was mental. Then we had our dueling music wars.

Kristen blasted Mariah Carey's "Dreamlover," super happy pop garbage that I counterbalanced with some Alice in Chains "Dirt" with its heavy guitars, droning vocal harmonies, and drug-induced lyrics. She fought back with Janet Jackson's insipid "That's the Way Loves Goes." Barf city. So I attacked with Soundgarden's "Jesus Christ Pose," thrashing guitars yet powerfully ethereal. She cued up some Ace of Base, and I rushed inside her room and turned off that nonsense.

"Like, don't you want to listen to music that has meaning?" I asked, my blood boiling. How could we come from the same womb and be such polar opposites?

Kristen was wearing a green facemask, her blond hair in a ponytail, ready for bed super early since she had a 6:00 a.m. track practice.

"Don't you ever want to listen to something that's not so depressing and moody?"

I started to respond that not all my favorite songs are depressing, but "Jesus Christ Pose" ended and "Face Pollution" began, making my point moot.

"I like songs about love," Kristen said.

"Mariah Carey is like artificial sweetener."

"Her songs are catchy," Kristen said. "Music doesn't have to open up a vein like you want it to."

"Will you just give, like, Nirvana a try?" I asked, begging. My eyes were even tearing, unsure why I was getting so emotional.

"Nico, it's just not for me."

"I'll play 'Drain You' and you'll see–"

"I have early practice tomorrow," she said, turning her nose to the door as an indication for me to leave. So I stomped out and turned my music up even louder, just to piss her off. The next day we didn't speak and the following morning after that she died so I could feel extra lousy about my shitty self.

• • •

I'm still high after leaving Winter's house and decide to just drive around and around as the sun sets beyond the hills coating the sky in orange and purple. I adjust the rearview mirror to apply my MAC Viva Glam Taupe Lipstick with brown lip liner and take a moment to assess myself. My hair has been dyed so many colors it appears clumpy and lifeless. The baby fat has finally fled from my cheeks, but my chin still looks weak (thanks Mom), unlike Dad or Kristen's strong jaw. My smile makes me resemble a chipmunk, and no one would ever call me beautiful, pretty maybe if I spend hours doing my makeup, but most likely, simply cute. Again, like a chipmunk.

I hit play on my mixtape and "Runaway Train" blasts. I roll up the windows so I can sing it loud without feeling embarrassed, belting the chorus that coincides with my upcoming journey, my flight to nowhere and everywhere at the same time. I've got the courage to run away now, but what would happen once I come down from my high? I'll likely curl up in bed to the sounds of In Utero, solely on my Walkman since Mom had freakin' broken my stereo.

I arrive home during Mazzy Star's luscious and mournful "Fade Into You." When I walk through the front door, Mom and Dad are waiting on opposite couches. Dad clears his throat.

"Park it, Scrap," he says, a nickname that used to be endearing when I was little, but now indicates how little he's involved in my life. I'm just a scrap to him, leftovers on a plate.

Dad has a sweep of silver hair that might have been called dashing like a movie star, but his tired, weighed-down eyes keep him ordinary. Winter once said that from far away he looks like Richard Gere in Pretty Woman and that she'd "do him." I responded by punching her in her big boob.

Mom gives a shy wave, as if we're old friends reuniting. I don't even bother to check if I give off a weed odor. Screw 'em both.

"I know about your mother and Mr. Ferguson," Dad says. He doesn't sigh like I expect him to; he explains their tryst like he's rattling off what we're having for dinner. "I have been seeing someone else as well. Annette."

I scrunch my face up. "Annette?" I picture some over-sexed French lady sharing my father's office cot after a boink session and feeding him escargot.

"Your mother and I are getting a divorce."

An image of Jeremy sashays into my thoughts, hands on hips, and an "I told ya so" pouring from his lips over and over. When I look at Mom, she gives a sobering nod.

"This is for the best, Nico," she says, and tries to grab my hand but I whip it away.

"I'll be staying with Annette at her place in Los Feliz," Dad continues. "You won't have to move."

"What if I don't want to live with her," I say, pointing at my mother like she's a defendant in a courtroom. That woman!

Mom chews on her lip. "Nico, we don't want to uproot you. And your father needs time to settle in."

"I don't wanna live with him either."

Finally, the two of them glance at each other, former opponents aligned against a new adversary.

"I'm gonna stay with Winter," I shout. "Her mom already said it's okay. They have an extra room."

"That's a big imposition," Dad barks, smoothing down his tie as if we're in a goddamn business meeting.

"I'll help around their house. Edina's practically begged me. And this isn't working out so we'll try it."

I stand up like I'm the parent who already made the decision. The allies, glance at each other again, neither willing to put up too much of a fight for me.

"O-kay," they both say in eerie harmony.

"I just need to pack," I say. "I'll be out of your hair tonight."

"Nico, there's no rush," my mom says. She stands up but just teeters in place, afraid to make a move.

I'm holding back tears, refusing to be emotional in front of them. I tell myself to be cold like Dad, a robot in flannel.

"Why waste any more time," I say, flapping my arms. "Like, we waste so much time all the time, ya know? And then one day..."

I mime the action of dropping dead and watch their faces scrunch up in response.

"So, it's been fun parental units. I'll call you in a few days when I'm settled too."

I spin around to head up the stairs. Out of the corner of my eye, I can see Mom try to come after me, but Dad raises his palm to hold her back. Am I not even worth an argument? I guess fucking not.

I dash into my room, get out a duffel bag, and throw in everything I think I'd need. My yellow Sports

Walkman and a shit ton of batteries. A dozen different band T-shirts and four practically identical flannels, a few various chokers, an off the shoulder leotard, two straight fit jeans, and two jeans shorts that I made by cutting up old pairs, some glitter nail polish, a couple of baby doll dresses, a Jansport backpack, some joints, my fake ID where my name is Sasha Lioni and I go to USC, a bag of makeup and hair dye, a Nirvana poster that I'd tape up in my car, and finally a picture of Kristen and I, nine and ten years old at camp on a trip up to Big Sur, the sun a bright melon ball making us squint, our arms around one another, smiles filled with braces, still innocent and unexposed to any tragedies.

On my way down, Dad meets me at the bottom of the stairs. He has his gas card in his hand.

"Use it as much as you need," he says, tucking it in my jeans pocket. He pats me on the shoulder. I can hear my mother sniffling in the kitchen. I keep my eyes trained on the floor and duck out of there, tossing the duffel bag in the passenger's seat and roaring off into the night.

• • •

I pull up to Winter's house, running on pure adrenaline, picturing the road spooling out before us as we crank out tunes and sing to the wind. I honk and honk until she emerges barefoot in an oversized sweatshirt, her toes freshly painted magenta, her white hair done up in cornrows.

"You and Jeremy ready, bee-yitch?" I yell, jumping

out and humping the hood of the car.

"Ssssshhh, Edina's got a migraine."

I zip my lips and shrug a "sorry."

"It's late, Nic," Winter says, already inching back toward the front door.

"Is Jeremy still here? C'mon, let's go! My dad even gave me his gas card. And they both bought that I'm moving in with you for a while."

"You're welcome to," Winter says, fishing through her pockets for a cigarette.

"No, we're running away," I yelp. "Remember?"

Winter looks out into the night and narrows her eyes.

"Go get Jeremy," I say, clapping for her to get a move on.

"Jeremy's passed out."

"So? I don't want to wait till tomorrow. Like, I'm amped up now."

"Yeah, Nico, listen..."

"Listen...? What are you talking about?" I get in her face. "Like, this is your idea."

She lets out a laughing smirk, a superior hint of how she'd break my heart.

"Nico, you know I talk out of my ass sometimes."

I shove her. "No! This is your idea. Running away. Screwing school. I'm all excited."

She ashes her cigarette on the sidewalk. "You should still totally go."

"You don't want to come with?" I ask, barely a mumble, my insides rumbling.

"I got Pearl Jam tickets. That boy Vince who I met in the music store is taking me. Remember?"

"No," I say, crossing my arms. "I can't keep track

of all your various dicks."

She smirks again. "Yeah, this has the potential of being a good one. And Pearl Jam is gonna be playing some new songs from their upcoming album."

"So what? They come to L.A. all the time. It's not a big deal."

She spits out her smoke at me. "You wouldn't be saying that if it was Nirvana."

"Screw you, Winter. You do this all the time. You promise one thing, but really mean something else. You're not real."

"What's that supposed to mean?"

"Like, I'm doing something. I made a plan. You have no plan. You'll just float forever."

She flicks her cigarette in my direction. The butt taps against my arm.

"Don't say anything you can't take back," she says. "You can be an exhausting friend, you know? Like, it's always about your up and down moods."

"I'm sorry my sister died and made me sad, Winter. We don't all get to live in happy hippie land with Edina."

"I go through my own shit too, Nic, but you, like, never care about what I'm dealing with. I had an abortion two months ago. Yeah, I did. But Jeremy and I decided we couldn't tell you because you need all the focus and the pity."

"What?" I say, my head spinning. "How could you not tell me that?"

"There's a lot I keep from you. Because you're made of glass and I'm afraid to be the one to make you shatter. Like, even with our monthly day of hooky to the Viper Room. It was never about River Phoenix. Each time, Jer and I are hoping you'd open up to us about Kristen, get you out of this depressing state."

"It's not a state. This is my life. I'll never not be depressed. I'm sorry to break it to you. That's why you should want to run away with me, so you could at least try to help me–"

"Exactly!" Winter chuckles. "Help you. What do you think I've been doing for the past six months? And did I once get a thank you?"

"Well, I'm just trying to survive these last six months and not take a knife to my wrists."

"You would never. You're just being dramatic."

We are screaming at each other now, our shrill voices echoing up the block. A light turns on downstairs in Winter's house and Jeremy steps outside rubbing his eyes.

"The whole block can hear you two," he says.

I run over and punch him hard in the shoulder.

"Owww," he cries, the true drama queen of our group.

"Screw you for not coming too." Tears are flying out now, my face flushed. "You two always just disappoint."

"We want you to go," Winter says, running her fingers through my hair, switching to her maternal self. "The truth is we would just get in the way."

I sit down on the edge of the curb and she inches up next to me, her head on my shoulder.

"You need to do this for yourself. Scratch off every item on your bucket list. Have an adventure."

"I'm scared," I say, as a chill wind whips through

the air, goosebumps springing up my neck.

"Just live, Nico," she says, as Jeremy flops down to the other side of me, hugging me tight too. "Show us that when Kristen died, you didn't die too. Because it's felt that way for a while now and that scares me."

I wipe away a hanging ball of snot and manage to nod.

"The three of us would kill each other if we all go," she continues. "It'd be a disaster. You know that. Have your adventure and come back and tell us everything."

"My parents are divorcing."

"Girl, who cares?" Jeremy adds. "That's on them. This is about you."

"When you come back, you can stay with me and Ed as long as you want," Winter says. "We'd love to have you. But I can't run away with you because I don't need to run away like you do, and neither does Jeremy. We're okay where we are, do you understand?"

I want to tell her that she drank too much and slept with too many dudes and is far from okay, and Jeremy's even worse, never having made a move on a guy even though he dreamed of it so. We are all brilliant messes. But instead I nod, too tired to argue, eager to get on the road and away from Laurel Canyon, away from even them.

I rise on shaky legs and meander back to the car.

"You call me anytime you need, Nico," Winter says. I can tell she feels guilty, but I let her stew in that. I open the door, slide inside, and turn on the ignition. "Runaway Train" comes up on the car speakers. I mouth the lyrics as Winter and Jeremy wave their goodbyes and blow kisses, and I feel more alone than ever. I wonder if once I leave if I'll ever come back, content to just drift into oblivion.

How on Earth did I get so jaded
Life's mystery seemed so faded

I warble the rest of the song quietly, clutching my bucket list in my fist as I steer with my other hand and embrace the dark road ahead that I figure I'd better get damn well used to.

4

• • • • •

Come As You Are - Nirvana

Aunt Carly, my dad's sister, lives up in Ojai in a house filled with crystals and what she likes to call "good energy." Ojai is like a natural and spiritual oasis full of hiking trails, pink moons, and eco-friendly neighbors where she fits right in. I arrive around midnight, knowing she'll probably still be up, a glass of red wine in hand, and deep in a book of poems. After Winter and Jeremy slayed me by backing out of the trip that was THEIR IDEA, I need Carly's positive aura before I take off solo. Carly's the only adult I know related to me who never judges and who actually listens. I'd held out seeking comfort for so long that my bones ache to be embraced.

A wind chime dances in front of her home, the doorbell playing what sounded like Enya. Carly teaches art at the local high school, letting music do the speaking in her classes, silent until the very end when a student would be ready to display their work. I imagine us painting watercolors on the porch while the sun rises.

The door swings open and sure enough, Aunt Carly stands there with a glass of red in one hand and a black and white cat in the other.

"Nico?" she says, eyes bugging out as she drops the cat and it trots off into the darkness of the street. She hugs me, spilling a dollop of red on my sleeve. When she pulls away, I long for more of her warmth. "Come in, come in."

Aunt Carly isn't the type to ask why I'm here so late, or if my parents know that I've come. She has a pretty bad relationship with my dad, the two of them even more polar opposites than me and Kristen. He resents her calm exterior, her scented oils, her love of psychedelics. She hates how he sold out to the man: his drive for money, his relationships relegated to lesser importance. The last time they saw each other, she had come down for Kristen's funeral and read from WB Yeats' poem, "Death".

Nor dread nor hope attend
A dying animal;
A man awaits his end
Dreading and hoping all;
Many times he died,
Many times rose again.

Aunt Carly left before the service at our house, likely not wanting to start a fight with Dad. When I went back up to my room after all the friends and relatives finally cleared out, a musty book of WB Yeats poems rested on my pillow with a note from Carly, saying "Words have the power to heal." Even though I'd rather choose Nirvana as my comforter, she was so right.

Stepping inside her place, I'm greeted by a trail of

variously colored cats, all of them mewling at this new stranger. I pick up an orange tabby.

"How many do you have now?" I ask, the tabby's whiskers tickling my face.

"They come and go," she says, her teeth stained wine-dark. "Just like everyone in my life. Happens as you get older."

She gives a wink, a joke between us. She seems more tired than the Aunt Carly I remember, but then I see a half-finished bottle of Merlot as the culprit.

"Pour yourself a glass and join me in the living room."

She floats away, her caftan disappearing around a corner. In her cramped kitchen, I run a dusty glass under the water and pour myself a hefty amount. I weave through glinting crystals dangling from the ceiling casting rainbow prisms. Her living room is a museum of her art: warped versions of the cats that slink around, painted in nuclear hues. The last time I was here years ago, she had an affinity for flowerbeds.

"I'm sorry I haven't been in touch, sweetness," she says, draping the caftan over her legs. The windows are open and Ojai gets cold at night, farther up north from Los Angeles, the mountains trapping in the heat during the day and setting it free in the evenings.

"I had an art show," she says, indicating the cat paintings. "Lots of prep work, and I can get so lost in creating. Sometimes I look up and a day or two has passed. I'm not teaching right now."

"I'm not in school right now either," I blurt out, already having chugged half my glass of wine. We cheers to that.

"It stifled me, ya-know, Nico? Not the students as much as the administration. They became so needling. They never supported my work."

She rests her chin on her fist and I observe how closely she and my father look alike, how much she resembles Kristen as well—but a warped version, much like her paintings. The California sun has made her skin leathery and freckly, not just tan but browned, muddy. She'd sewn feathers into her beachy curls, her wrists jangling with crystals, her voice light and airy.

"I've been feeling stifled too," I say, at ease with being honest around Carly, ready to tell her why I've come. So I do.

She responds with a sip of wine and an approving nod.

"I ran away once too," she replies. "As you know, my father, your grandfather died quite young. He and my mother had us when they were still teenagers. He passed while my mother was still in the hospital with me."

"I know," I say, swearing I could feel my brain throb.

"My mother and I never got along. She found God after our father's death and I just couldn't relate once I became old enough to think on my own. Sure, I followed her brimstone for a while, but when I was fourteen, I hightailed it out of there. Joined a commune. Right up here in Ojai. Lived here ever since."

"I didn't know that," I say, clutching my glass. I'm starting to get sleepy.

"That's part of why your father and I don't get along. He was stuck with Norma Sullivan, her blessed little boy. I was the devil child who managed to escape.

Frankly, it's time for him to let that go."

She chugs the rest of her glass like a sorority girl and then holds it out to me to get her more. I leap over darting cats and grab the bottle from the kitchen. When I come back inside, she's leaning over her record player.

"We should have some music," she says, shaking her bony hips.

I expect her to put on some hippy-dippy tunes, similar to what Edina liked. I wish she'd be my cool mom like Winter gets to have. I'm surprised when Nirvana's "Come As You Are" slinks through the air instead. Its sound droning, menacing, needy, Cobain's wail desperate and pleading to not be judged.

"I didn't realize you're into Nirvana," I say, smiling for the first time since I left L.A.

"I remember seeing all of their posters in your room. I'd heard about the band, sure, and figured I should check 'em out. They're not the Beatles, but every generation has their own ideas of gods."

We sway along to Cobain's growl, and I picture his beer-laced breath breathing life into me. When the song ends, she lowers the volume so Cobain becomes a whisper and we fall onto the couch.

"So, this bucket list," Aunt Carly says, poking me on the shoulder. "What's on it?"

"Oh, you know, typical teenage wishes."

I whip it out of my pocket and pass the crumpled page over.

Nico's Supa Fly Bucket List

```
                    Learn Guitar
Climb a High Mountain and Get Over My
```

Fear of Heights
Sleep Under the Stars in the Wilderness
Go Surfing
See Seattle and the Real Grunge Scene
Give Back to Nature in Some Form
Kiss a Boy I REALLY Like
Go to Kurt Cobain's House
Push Aside Courtney Love And Maul My Hero
Get Front Row Seats to Nirvana in Concert
Sing In Front of a Real Audience (not just in the shower)

Carly pops up to her feet. "Ooooooohhhhh." She shuffles out of the room and comes back with a large backpack. "This has a sleeping bag, rain gear, a Ziploc bag of trail mix and granola, and a flint and a pop tent all ready to go."

She tosses it on the seat next to me.

"Nico, Ojai has some of the best camping in the nation. That's why you came here."

"I didn't even think of that, I just wanted to hang out with you for the night."

"Nonsense, your subconscious willed you here to begin your adventure. In the morning, I'll take you to Ojai Meadows Preserve and you can check that first item off the list."

My stomach rumbles, the wine the only thing I'd ingested since that salami and cheese sandwich for lunch. While I should've been excited, I actually am afraid.

"I can see that troubled look on your face, Nico. This is a wonderful mission that you're on and you need to see it through. You'll begin under the stars. It will be revolutionary!"

"You think?"

I haven't told her that I'm really doing all this, because I'm worried my fate would eventually align with Kristen's. I'd only mentioned about the 'rents divorcing and how they'd pissed me off. But Aunt Carly has a sixth sense, a talent for being a spiritual detective. I can tell she knows the real reason.

"Kristen was a lovely soul," she says, the life draining from her face. I imagine that's how I look when I'd mention my sister. "I remember when she was born. She glowed. Your father and I were on little better terms then. I cried at this little golden nugget that fit in the palm of my hand. I thought of all the amazing things ahead of her in life. Our existences are far from fair."

I rub my eyes, sadness defeating sleep. I'm tired of crying.

"You want to do everything she couldn't, don't you?" Aunt Carly says. She nods her head, telling me it's a fact.

I agree because it's easier than speaking about my fear of following Kristen's footsteps. Carly would just tell me how crazy that is like everyone else, even though I can feel the rotting already occurring, this treacherous takeover of my brain.

"Oh, love," Carly coos, and lets me rest my head on her chest. She combs my hair with her long painter's fingers. "We all face tragedies. It's how we surface from them, which shows us who we really are. Dreaming under the stars will do you well. I do it all the time when I crave an exorcism."

"An exorcism?"

"The demons inside of you, the monsters who bring you down. They always exist, sometimes there's just more of them than other times. That's when you need to take action."

"Okay," I say, touching one of the feathers in her hair. "I'll go."

"Delightful. Nico, I see so much of myself in you."

"Really?"

"Oh yes, we are old souls and aliens too. We're not entirely built for this Earth."

I look over at the Merlot bottle and see it's empty, likely the cause of Aunt Carly veering off the rails.

"And others like to judge us," she continues. "They point and stare. They cast us aside. They are afraid of what they cannot fit in a little boring box. But that's why we're superior. We understand the necessity to weave outside the lines."

She spins her hands through the air as her audience of cats watches in awe.

"But between you and I, they're all jealous. We'll find the secret one day because we are on the right train, the one that's invisible to practically everyone else."

"Have you found the secret?" I ask. My breath is practically caught in my throat, my heart thumping away.

She looks to the left and then to the right as if she's being watched. Finally, she blinks her eyes to confirm.

"And you will too," she says. "You'll see the sign and never feel alone again."

She reaches for the bottle and notices that she has killed it. She shrugs her shoulders in response.

"That means it's bedtime. I rise at sunrise every morning, sweet Nico. I'll wake you just when the light emerges and we'll watch it soar together."

She rises and wobbles to her bedroom, her trail of cats following, her caftan sparkling against the dangling crystals that separate her bedroom.

I kick off my Doc Martins, wrapping myself in a throw blanket, lulled to sleep by Cobain's painful lithium warbles.

• • •

With a rooster's crow, Aunt Carly rustles me from sleep just before dawn. We stumble out onto her porch, steaming coffee mugs in hand. The sky opens up and a fireball rises, spreading brilliant reds and oranges across the land. I realize I'd never seen the sunrise before and neither of us spoke while it continues its path upward. A few cats join us, rubbing against legs, prowling in the warming and tickling light. The mountains create a backdrop, a frame for this perfect painting. Aunt Carly brings out sheets of paper and with Cray Pas crayons we capture the moment: my drawing childish, hers beautiful. She rolls it up and tucks it in my waistband.

"To take on your travels so I'm with you too."

Her eyes crinkle along with a smile. I blink and see Kristen in her place, an older, middle-aged Kristen, one who survived the attack on her brain, who'd been able to put it behind her. Two sisters watching the sunrise, long past squabbling over the different sizes of our rooms and that we could only bond over our parents' annoying habits. Sisters who'd never be friends, but closer than I'd ever be with Winter or Jeremy because we'd be locked for life and always have each other's back.

"Are you ready to truly see the stars?"

Carly's voice startles me since it isn't Kristen's. I wouldn't go through life with a sister who'd always have my back. Like Aunt Carly says, people would come and go, and I'd better get used to it.

We drive in her purple Geo Prism to Ojai Meadows Preserve. Aunt Carly says she'll hold onto my duffel bag so I won't have too much to carry. She will return in twenty-four hours to pick me up. She doubts my dad would call her asking my whereabouts, and I tell her I have it covered with my friend, Winter. My tongue trips over saying "friend," usually referring to Winter as a "best friend." Right then, I honestly feel like she doesn't deserve my friendship. I wonder how things would be between Winter and me when I'd return, and I realize I don't f-ing care.

Aunt Carly gives me a map of the area with the best spot to camp. She says that I should be open to meeting other travelers or having this experience on my own if that's what meant to be.

"Don't overthink any of these experiences you'll be having," she says, chewing on a blade of grass. "Just be."

"I will. Thanks, Carly."

We hug. When I hold on for an extra moment, she lets me.

I jump outside and the car immediately drives away,

like she's afraid I'll chicken out and beg her to take me back. She's right. I look around and don't see anyone, never being so alone to such an extent before. It seems like I'm the only girl on the planet right there, an alien beamed down, just like Aunt Carly, knees knocking together as I hike up a pathway. I take out my Sports Walkman and fast-forward until I find "Come As You Are," wondering what nature has in store for me and if this crazy idea of running away would start off wonderful, or if I'm about to be doused with mud and soaked in bleach like Cobain sings.

I know no matter what, he'll welcome me like he always seems to do with his divine and brutal rasp.

5

• • • • •

Stargazer – Mother Love Bone

It's hella hot out hiking through the Preserve, the cool sun my sworn enemy. The ball of fire I'd loved earlier that morning gets the brunt of my middle finger now. Birds sing along on my jaunt like I'm a princess in a Disney film, except my pale and sunburned ass must've looked like a heaving lobster clawing its way through the wetlands. I'd brought along a Polaroid camera, promising myself I'd take a picture to mark each bucket list item, so I snap a shot of majestic scenery: a craggy mountain with puffs of green trees at the base. I think about Winter and Jeremy and what it would've been like if they had run away with me too. Winter would be complaining about her sweaty big boobs being constricted by her bra, and Jeremy would be convincing us to do this hike wasted. I burp up the wine from last night and figure that's enough of a buzz for the time being. Just in case, I've got a spare joint tucked in my jeans shorts.

While I walk, I whip out my spiral notebook with

a purple-haired Cobain looking spooked on the cover, probably wondering why the hell anyone cared enough to take a picture of him. Sometimes I write lyrics, but I've never finished a whole song. In hot pink scribble, the title stares back at me. Nico's Lament. I get a burst of inspiration.

Spiral to vanish
Ebb of the tide flows strong
Dark beneath the blue
Ice between my toes
Circling fishes give up hope

Just like that inspiration vanishes, and I stuff the notebook back inside.

After about two hours, I wrench off my giant backpack and nibble on a PBJ sandwich Aunt Carly made for me—organic peanut butter and jelly of course. It tastes like sweet wallpaper, but I'm hungry so I gobble it up. After I finish, I'm not ready to continue hiking so I take out my Walkman. Mother Love Bone's "Stargazer" fills up the expansive space. While they aren't my favorite band—ahem, Nirvana—I like that not every average schmuck knows who they are. Mother Love Bone is the band you mention when you'd go to a party with college guys attending, just to impress them—that's what Winter and I decided. I wonder if Winter is with her music store dude and if they're boning. I tell myself to forget about her and stop living as if the two of us share the same life because we clearly don't.

Since I don't see anyone around, I start to sing along to the song. I close my eyes and imagine myself in front of a large crowd swaying with lighters in hand. In this vision, I don't appear as a lobster but as the best version of myself: the cool chick that guys want to be with and girls want to be. A rockstar. An idol whose voice doesn't go silent when others are watching. The lyrics float from my lips and speak to my listeners. Warms their souls. Stirs their hearts. Uplifts them when life seems cruel. Exactly like what music does for me. The eternal shoulder to lean on.

I feel a tap on my actual shoulder and swivel around, ready to bite whoever's hand it is.

"What?" I snap, unplugging one headphone from my ear. I expect to see some roly-poly park ranger chastising me for doing something not so eco-friendly. To my surprise, a hot guy stands in place of my expectations. He looks like a mix of Matt Dillon from Drugstore Cowboy and Singles. Hella yum. I curl my fried hair behind my ear and shyly smile.

"Sorry," he says, throwing up his palms. "Didn't mean to scare you."

"Haha, you didn't, haha."

Stop laughing like an idiot, you idiot, I warn myself.

"I heard you singing," he says, shoving his hands in his pockets. His eyes are brown like the buttons on a corduroy jacket I once had, his smile crooked and sexy, his arms wiry and long. "Big Mother Love Bone fan here."

"Oh yeah, haha." I throw back my head, cackling like a maniac. "They don't get the respect they deserve."

He steps closer and I melt, wanting his wiry arms to squeeze the life out of me. Honestly craving any type of touch right now.

"I know, everyone at my school is so into Nirvana

and Pearl Jam, but they're both so mainstream."

"So mainstream," I say, giving my true idol the thumbs down and then immediately feeling guilty for doing so. I picture Cobain shaking his head and murmuring "poser" under his breath. "Where do you go to school?"

"Kenbo High," he says, looking off into the distance. "So do my friends that I'm with." He nods over to a massive rock where I can vaguely see a few shapes and shadows intermingling. "It sucks balls. But I'll apply somewhere good for college once I get my grades up. High school is, like, too much pot and girls."

"Oh, haha, same. I mean, same to the pot, switch the girls to boys."

I'm impressed with how chill I'm acting. Pat on the back for Nico.

"Where do you go?"

"It's in L.A.," I say, and without missing a beat, "I'm Sasha Lioni." I'm ready to be someone else right now. Unburdened Sasha who's not running away from her dead sis.

"Oh cool," he says, extending his hand. His is warm. "I'm Gregg with two g's. Actually, three g's."

"Greggggggggg," I hum, dragging out his name that feels good on my tongue.

"Do you want to join us, Sasha? We brought guitars and are about to shred. Or did you want to be alone?"

I take a second to make my decision, even though I'm already getting tired of myself and my thoughts. Gregg with three g's seems like a perfect distraction.

"Nah, shredding sounds hella good."

We walk over to his friends. Gregg wants to study

marine biology, and I say that I'm still undecided. He asks if I'd consider music, but I shrug that off and reply that I'm just planning on trying out every subject.

"I dig it, Sasha."

"Who?" I say, and then laugh like a crazy person, hoping I'd covered my slip-up.

We meet Gregg's friends, two crunchy girls named Jessa and Lisette, a white and a Spanish girl both with dreadlocks and enough piercings to give Hellrazer a run for his money. He also has a buddy Jimmy, who stares only at my breasts when he speaks to me.

"I'm up here," I say, pointing to my face. Jimmy seems baked, his eyes spinning like Winter's would when she'd get extra sloppy.

"Burn," Gregg says, punching Jimmy in the shoulder. "Ignore Jimmy, Sasha. He's as high as a fly."

"Aren't we gonna jam, man?" Jimmy asks. He takes out his guitar and starts noodling around.

Jessa and Lisette agree. "Sasha, can you play?" Jessa asks, picking at her nose ring.

"Sasha can sing!" Gregg cheers. "I heard her before belting out Mother Love Bone's 'Stargazer'."

"I know that one," Lisette says. She takes off the leather jacket she must've been roasting in and begins to play. She isn't super talented. I can't get lost in the music, but she's serviceable, I guess.

"I don't really wanna sing," I say, shriveling up in place. "Like, I usually sing when I'm alone."

"That's no fun," Jimmy says, and shoots a snot rocket from his nose onto the rock.

"Jimmy, you are, like, so gross," Jessa says.

"But baby, you like it," he replies and mock-tackles

her until they're wrestling and swapping spit.

"They do that all the time," Gregg says, shaking his head. "What about the guitar? You can play mine."

He holds out a beautiful acoustic guitar filled with stickers of Mudhoney, Fugazi, Faith No More, and Mother Love Bone.

"I can't play."

"I'll teach you," Gregg says. He has a smooth way of talking, each word dipped in cool. I look over at Lisette and see she's frowning. She probably wants Gregg to be teaching her. Sorry, girl, you snooze, you freakin' lose.

"Yeah, teach me how to play 'Stargazer'."

We inch our butts down the rock, leaving Lisette with Jessa and Jimmy who are about to conceive a baby in front of us all. Gregg wipes away the dirt for me to sit. Even though there's just more dirt under what he wiped away, I appreciate the gesture. He talks about chords, how 'Stargazer' starts with G and C and then the chorus is F and G. I hold the guitar in my lap as his hands direct my fingers from G and C. He softly sings the lyrics under his breath as I strum.

"You're a natural!" he says, his smile even more crooked than before. I like a boy who knows how to flirt well.

"You're just saying that."

"Not at all. It's because you can sing. Singers have a musical ability in them so they're usually good at instruments too."

He moves my hands until they are playing F and G. I crane my neck and stare at him as I strum. We shift so I'm leaning against his chest, his legs splayed so I could fit in between.

"You could be a model," he whispers into my ear, his lips touching my earlobe.

"No way, Jose," I say. "I have a cake-loving body that isn't made for starving."

"You have curves, Sasha." He mimes my curves through the air. I've never had a boy refer to my body in that way. I've never even thought of my body like that: curvy as opposed to porky.

"Those two up there, Lisette and Jessa, they're so stick thin, it's like grabbing onto nothing. I like meat."

"Glad to hear you're a carnivore, too."

He blinks his eyes confused.

"It means meat-eater, haha."

"I know that. I do plan on going to college, remember?"

He pushes back his mane of black hair, tucking it in place behind his ears. He has a scar over his lip that I point at.

"How'd you get that?"

"My lip scar? Knife fight in the wilds of Ojai. Nah, this cat on a farm scratched through my lip when I went to say hi to it one morning. Stupid pussy, right?"

"Pussies are so stupid," I say, smirking. He's slowly leaning in closer, his mouth already opening for a kiss. The last guy I'd made out with had been this burnout named Zane, who was never without his skateboard at school and liked to do Special K and go into a K hole. He was always uncertain what day it was and his tongue tasted like ashes. It was a hookup I didn't even tell Winter or Jeremy about.

Gregg, however, tastes sweet and minty, as if he'd

been planning our make-out sesh from the jump.

"Greggers," a voice yells from above. Jimmy's dumb head pops over the edge of the rock, his hair covering his face and looking like Cousin It. "Ready to smoke some chronic?"

Gregg lets out a roar in response. "Hell yeah! You into that, Sasha?"

I'd never done chronic before, but I certainly wasn't a newbie in terms of marijuana. The sun heads toward the West, setting soon. The thought of losing my mind in the wilderness too rad to pass up.

"Yeah, let's do it," I say, figuring I'd already learned guitar, an item on my bucket list I can mentally check it off. So now it's time to celebrate like a rock star.

• • •

The chronic is way more intense than I expect it to be. After a moment of freaking out because I think my teeth are made of broken glass, Gregg calms me down and plays Mother Love Bone's "Stargazer."

"Look at the stars, Sasha. 'Where is your star? Is it far, is it far, is it far? When do we leave? I believe, yes, I believe'."

I lie back with my head propped under my flannel shirt and stare at the sky, which seems like it's exploding. In Laurel Canyon, we definitely have a great view of the solar system but not like this. I'd never known how many stars crowded the night, so far away but seeming like I could pluck and place them on my tongue. I try but miserably fail.

Gregg stops playing "Stargazer" and leans over me

instead. He gives me a long tongue-filled kiss that tastes like grass this time instead of mint.

"You're so hot, Sasha."

"Mmmm, you too."

I feel my shorts being pulled to my ankles and then tossed to the sky.

"Is this okay?" he asks. "I just want you."

"Where's everyone else?" I ask, looking around and seeing nothing but nature, Gregg and I entering our own delicious world.

"Frolicking off on their own," he says. "I don't care about them. I like you, Sasha."

"I like you too."

I'm wearing a Soundgarden T-shirt that magically comes off. His hands fumble with my bra.

"Can I take off your bra?" he asks, already unhooking, his hands cupping my breasts. His fingers are so electric. "I know we're messed up. I don't want you to do anything you don't want to do."

"Just shut up and do it already," I say, kissing him so he'd stop talking. I'm just ready to feel something, someone, anything—if only for a shimmering moment. Colors dance around us. A comet soars overhead. He nibbles on my nipple, his mouth full of sparks, and then reaches down into my panties, his long index finger further reaching inside. My orgasm echoes throughout the land.

I'd slept with a few guys after the disaster with Jeremy, none of them more than once, each one while I was inebriated. I wonder how sex is sober, but that would clearly not happen tonight. Gregg is inside of me, squirming around, calling out my fake name to an audience of curious animals who cock their heads to the side watching our theatrics. Tucked in between them I spy Kristen and nearly lose my shit, but it's not a fully formed Kristen, more ethereal than real.

"Who is this loser?" Kristen's ghost asks. She doesn't seem pleased, crossing one arm over the other like she used to do when I'd inevitably say something stupid.

I try to look away but her ghost pops over into my line of sight, refusing to be ignored.

"He could have an STD, Nico!" Kristen snaps. And then she starts to list them all. When she gets to the Clap, I stick my fingers in my ears and yell, "La, la, la, la, la."

This makes Gregg think I'm super into him, so he starts pumping harder and it's over in what feels like seconds. Kristen's ghost has vanished and I already miss her chastising, wondering if it had only been the intense weed that sorta made her return. Gregg apologizes for coming so fast saying we could try it again, but the pot is like wayyyy kicking in now. His hair is standing straight up and he turns into a vision of Don King, Mike Tyson's manager with the crazy hair. I laugh like a hyena, and his insecure ass thinks I'm laughing at his lack of sexual sustainment.

"Are you making fun of me?" Don King asks.

"No, no way. You're Don King and all the animals just watched us boink."

"What?"

"What?"

"Spoon with me," he says, wrapping his elongated arms around me so I can't break free. He breathes hot spurts of air into the back of my neck. Had we even used a condom? No wonder Kristen showed up. I think of Winter's abortion confession and worry if that might be an unfortunate item to add to my bucket list. It'd certainly sour this trip.

"That was so hot," he says, and then says it again. I pretend I'm sleeping. When he finally passes out, I weasel out of his grasp and flee into the darkness until I can't see my hands in front of me anymore. I disappear. I am invisible. Luckily, I've brought my Walkman so I cue up "Stargazer" again, letting the song fill the entire Earth until its lead singer Andrew Woods' lyrics are all that exists.

• • •

I wake up to Lisette standing over me screaming, "whore" into my face. Apparently, Gregg is her man and I'm some little floozy that came between them. He'd confessed to her that he'd fallen for me. She rifles through my backpack and is throwing trail mix. Once an almond hits me in the eye, I've had enough.

"I don't want your man, nutjob," I say. "I need to go."

"You slutty girls are all the same," Lisette spits. "Gregg and I are in love."

"Obviously not."

"You seduced him."

"Your man is capable of making his own decisions and he likely wants to get away from a psycho like you."

She punches me, not like a girl with a weak fist. She makes good contact with my cheek. I can feel it already getting red and throbbing. I leap at her and get out my claws. This is not my first rodeo in the ring. Eventually, she starts yelling for everyone to get me off her. Gregg and Jimmy grab me by the arms, lifting me away.

"I think you should go, Sasha," Gregg mumbles, refusing to look me in the eye.

I stick my tongue into my cheek to see how badly it hurts. "Yeah, as fast as I can."

"I loved last night," he whispers, after making sure that Lisette couldn't see his confession.

"It was okay," I say, brushing myself off. Cuckoo Lisette had gotten my clothes all dirty. "And Kurt Cobain is amazing by the way. Anyone who can't see that is too clueless to breathe."

I grab everything from the backpack that Lisette had spilled out and stuff it inside.

"If you ever come back," Lisette says, "I will cut you."

"Ojai sucks," I yell in response, giving them all the middle finger.

It's a two-hour walk back to where Aunt Carly would be picking me up. I nibble on some granola and run to her Geo Prism when I see it. Jumping inside, I take a whiff of my armpits and decide I smell like spoiled milk.

"Did you see the stars, Nico?" Aunt Carly asks. One of her cats sits in her lap, its paws on the wheel like it's driving too.

"I learned guitar, boned a dude who's cheating on his nutbar girlfriend, and yeah, saw a brilliant showing of stars. That was honestly the best part."

I leave out seeing Kristen's specter, wisely keeping that vision to me, myself, and I.

"Good, baby," Aunt Carly says, leaning over and kissing me on the cheek, already smelling of wine. "Where's your next stop?"

I don't have an answer for her, but I figure I'll make my way to Cobain's place in Seattle like my bucket list decrees so somewhere toward Northern California would be my next destination.

"I'm so sleepy, Carly, can I just listen to some music while we get outta here?"

She shrugs her shoulders and puts her foot on the gas. I plug in my headphones and cue up the mix I'd made for Kristen. As "F**k and Run" by Liz Phair blasts in my eardrums, I hum along.

From up above, Kristen is likely continuing to chastise my poor decisions, whispering to God that I'm getting further and further away from how I should be behaving. But prim and pristine Kristen probably should've had more boning sessions in her short life, so I pretend she's thinking of doing that instead.

Good on you, Nico. No lasting relationships that could be taken away from you as quickly as a short breath. Fuck and run, fuck and run, till only your footprints would be left behind as a reminder.

6

• • • • •

Today – Smashing Pumpkins

Just outside of San Luis Obispo, roughly halfway between L.A. and San Francisco, the Smashing Pumpkins "Today" comes up on Kristen's mixtape. I'm not in the mood to hear about today being the greatest day I'd ever known. I had driven straight from Ojai after saying bye to Aunt Carly and her army of cats, and now I'm fully alone. I have the scary thought of no one being aware of where I am, drifting off into nothingness, my body washing up ashore on some rando beach, the headline labeling me Runaway Train Meets Her End. In heaven, Kristen would frown at my unspectacular demise, my wasted life. At least I would've taken it into my own hands rather than leave it up to that sneaky bastard, Fate.

It's late afternoon, and I ache to talk to Winter. I want to hold out and make her realize how much she took our friendship for granted, but I'm honestly too weak. I need a taste of home so I drive into San Luis Obispo and find the first telephone booth.

"Yello?" Winter says.

"It's me...."

She takes a breath before responding. "Nico, where are you?"

"San Luis Obispo."

"How's the runaway going?"

"I learned guitar, did some chronic in Ojai, and messed around with a guy whose girlfriend clocked me in the face."

"Gnarly."

I picture Winter lying back in bed, her feet planted against a Pearl Jam poster, wrapping the phone cord around her index finger.

"So, yeah, running away has been great," I say, choking on a ball of phlegm, the tears beginning.

"Good to hear," she mumbles.

"Why did you do this to me?" I finally ask.

Sigh. "Nico, I set you free."

"You bailed–"

"You never would've gone! Look, you wanna bitch at me go ahead and say whatever you want, but the next time I might not pick up when you call."

"I've never felt so alone," I say. A cool wind makes the goosebumps spring up along my arms. I unravel my flannel from around my waist and put it on.

"You always have me, Nic."

"Obviously not."

"You do. We're closer than sisters can be, that's why I can tell you the truth."

"Which is?"

"If you stayed in L.A. something bad would've happened to you. I could feel it. You were headed for an explosion."

"What makes you think I still won't?"

"You probably will. It's called hitting rock bottom. But then there's nowhere to go but up."

"You sound like a self-help guru."

"I'm not ready for my rock bottom yet, but maybe someday I'll get my act together. Someday when we're able to go to Mars."

"What makes you think I'm ready?"

A long silence hangs between us, the crackle of her voice sounding so far away.

"Because I don't think you'll survive if you don't. Sometimes we stand at a precipice, the choice to go one way or another. This is your moment. Don't be swallowed up by your shitty past, fall into an awesome future."

I have a vision of myself falling off a mountain, breaking the speed barrier as I rush to my doom.

"I never knew Kristen well...." Winter begins. Hearing her name feels like my heart is put in a vice. "She didn't like me, I know that. Winter: the bad influence. But one time I came over and you weren't home yet and the two of us hung out."

"You never told me this."

"I'm telling you now. We were in her room full of trophies and stupid Ace of Base posters, and she said something I'll never forget."

"What?" I gasp.

"She said she envied me. I looked at her screwy, thinking she's messing with me. Evidently, I was the free spirit she could never be. Her existence was based on good grades and being captain of the track and field team, but beyond that, she had no clue who she was. That was all she said about it. It was as if I'd caught her talking to herself. That's why when you brought up your bucket list, I knew you wouldn't be doing it just for yourself, you're doing it for her as well. She should be the one running away with you now, not me. Get it?"

I stare at the fairly empty street: a few shops closing for the day, a car waiting at the stoplight, a woman whose hat gets caught by the breeze.

"I love you, Nico. I don't want you to be mad at me."

"I'm not," I say, imagining Kristen outside of the phone booth. She gestures to hurry up so we can go. Now I know why she showed up before in Ojai. "I understand," I tell Winter the Wise.

"Good." I hear the sound of her sucking at a cigarette or a joint. "So this girl's guy who you messed around with, was he hot?"

"He looked like Matt Dillon."

"Score one for Nico. Good in bed?"

"Yeah, for all of a minute."

"Ah, a preemie."

"I guess. How's your music store guy?"

"Oh yeah, the Pearl Jam concert rocked. They played a ton off of Vs. And Vince, yeah he's cool, I guess. Cool enough to see again. Plus he has a big wang."

"Aces."

"Oh, your parents called to talk to Edina and she totally covered for you. They say to hit them up in a few days."

"Thank Edina for me."

"She's glad to do it. Always thought your parents

were kind of twats anyway."

This makes me laugh. I hear a click, meaning the call is about to end if I don't add more coins.

"I gotta go, Winter."

"You should totally head to Pismo Beach by San Luis Obispo, I heard it's great. Didn't you tell me once that you want to try surfing? Find a beach boy to show you how."

"Yeah, good idea. I'll do that."

"All right, Nic Nic, take over the world for me."

I hear another click and the call ends, Winter's voice slowly fading away. A colder breeze blows by with the scent of the ocean, so I get back into my car to go spend the night by the waves.

• • •

Sleeping in my car for the night is colder than I expect. I have to wear three flannels with another as a blanket. I pretend Kristen is snoozing beside me so I can share her body heat, and it pretty much works. I nestle into her blond hair, her Sunflowers perfume replacing the Odor Eater dangling from the rearview.

"I'm so cold," I whisper to her. She looks back at me as if I don't even know what true cold can be. "But you're not a cadaver now," I say. "You're here."

I link my fingers with hers like we used to do when we were very little and I wouldn't be able to tell whose were whose as if we shared the same body.

"Right? You're here?" I ask again, my bowels rumbling at the thought that she might just vanish.

She nods. "You're not alone on this trip, Brenda."

A private joke between us. A frozen tear trickles into my mouth.

In the morning, a tangerine sun spreads its warmth and I step out, the blazing sand between my toes. I throw out some Taco Bell wrappers from last night's dinner, take a piss behind a carefully concealed bush, and watch the early morning surfer boys catching the best waves.

Yesterday, I had turned off "Today" by the Pumpkins when I wasn't ready for it, but I'm able to handle the lyrics better now. Each day really is limitless, anything could happen, and I want to make each one as amazing as possible for Kristen. She'd be counting on me.

One boy, in particular, seems to catch each wave he attempts. He's lean with short, dark hair and tan skin, probably weighing less than me. After about an hour, he tucks his surfboard under his arm and splashes up on shore.

Say something to him, dummy, I tell myself, as he makes his way closer. I wave like a fool. Instead of looking at me strangely, he waves back.

"You're really good out there," I say. "You caught pretty much every wave."

"You a surfer, too?" he asks. A giant cross hangs from his neck, silver and sparkling.

"Aspiring. Just getting some inspiration."

He plunges the surfboard into the sand, so it stands upright.

"Ever try?"

I shake my head. "Never had someone offer to teach me."

"It's all about having the right teacher." He extends his hand. "I'm Stephen."

Unlike Gregg with three g's, Stephen doesn't exude a trying-to-be cool attitude. Gregg tried too hard to impress, but really was lame. Stephen seems like he doesn't care what other people think.

"Nico," I say, not bothering with an alias this time.

"Nico? Never heard a name like that before."

"It's short for Nicole, but there are too many Nicoles out there. I like being the only Nico."

"Mission accomplished then. You go to SLO High, never seen you before?"

"No, I live in L.A. Just taking a road trip."

"Oh wow, on your own?" he asks, his voice awkwardly rising. "That takes a lot of guts."

I rub my stomach. "Well, I got 'em."

He laughs at that, even though the joke is corny as hell.

"You're funny, Nico. I got plans in a little with some friends, but you want to try to catch a wave?"

"The water's too cold and I don't have a wetsuit."

"I got an extra one in my car. If you want to, that is. I just love seeing someone catch a wave for the first time. Makes my year."

Stephen smiles a lot. After everything he says, he opens his mouth wide enough to show me his back molars.

"C'mon, Nico," he says, helping me up. "There are few perfect waves left this morning before the ocean settles."

We go to Stephen's car that has bumper stickers all relating to God. A Jesus fish stands out amongst others, along with a quote that says, "But Jesus beheld them, and says unto them, With men this is impossible; but with God all things are possible."

"God spelled backward is dog," is all I could think of saying.

"I see you noticed my bumper stickers."

"You like a missionary or something?"

"No, I mean, I do volunteer for my Christian Youth Organization." He stops smiling for once. "Most people who aren't into it seem to judge."

"I'm judged all the time," I say, wiping my brow as if it's exhausting being me. "Like, what did you think of me when you first saw me?"

"See I don't judge people before I meet them. I let their actions show me who they are."

"Jesus would approve."

"Is that a joke?"

"It is, but I didn't mean to offend you or anything. I just haven't met anyone so into God before, like, you don't exist in L.A."

"I'll take that as a compliment." His smile is back, teeth shiny in the sunlight. He opens his car and passes me a wetsuit. "There's a bathroom right there so you can change."

"Oh, I didn't realize they were public. Thanks."

I head over and put on the wetsuit, then meet him out front of the bathrooms. I'm a little embarrassed since the wetsuit is skintight and reveals every possible bulge. I don't feel his eyes looking me up and down.

"Ready to see God?" he asks.

"What?"

"Just kidding, Nico. I can be funny too."

We practice "popping up" before we head into the water. Stephen would say, "pop up" while I lie on my stomach next to the surfboard. Then I'd push myself up so I can land my feet on the surfboard.

"Good job," he says, with a thumbs up. "Not everyone can do that."

"I'm sure most people can."

"You'd be surprised. Ready for the real thing?"

I stare at the unruly ocean tide, imagining I'd be swallowing a lot of saltwater.

It takes many faulty starts of Stephen yelling, "pop up" as a wave would come in. I push myself up only to flail back into the water, far from a graceful swan.

"You keep psyching yourself out," he says. "You don't believe you can do it."

You can, I heard Kristen's voice say. Some of those sports genes had to go to you too. I couldn't have gotten all of them.

"Nico, when I say 'pop up' the next time, don't picture yourself wiping out, tell yourself that your feet will land on the surfboard and you'll glide."

My teeth are chattering. "Okay."

We watch a wave trickle closer. Through clogged ears, I hear Stephen yell, "pop up." As if hands from above have joined the party, I'm carried onto the surfboard and fly along with the wave. It lasts only a few seconds, but it's more of a high than any drug or drink I've ever had. My heart beats so fast I think it'll shoot out of my chest to get eaten up by the fishes. I direct myself to shore where I giggle like a little kid. Stephen meets up with me and I leap into his arms, dangling from his neck.

"That was amazing!" I say.

"I can tell."

I go to kiss him, but he turns his cheek. I'm running on too much adrenaline to care.

"More, more, more," I scream.

"I'd love to stay here all day, but I'm meeting some friends. We're hiking up Bishop Peak. Perfect day for it."

"I loooooove mountains," I shout, even though I'd honestly rather get my nails pulled out than deal with heights. This is a new Nico, however. She faces her stupid fears.

"Really? Okay, do you want to come along? They're both friends from my Christian Youth Organization."

"Does Jesus have holes in his hands?" I ask, trying to be funny.

"What?"

"Of course I want to come, Stephen. I'm having so much fun with you."

I run a finger down his arm, flirting to the max. He inches away, shy to the max. I like the challenge.

"O...kay, do you have a change of clothes?" he asks.

"My car's right over there," I reply, gesturing to the distance.

"Cool, we can get out of these smelly wetsuits and you could follow me there."

"Hella dope. And thanks, Stephen. So far, today is the greatest day I've ever known."

I can tell he doesn't recognize the Pumpkins reference.

"Every day is the greatest day I've ever known," he replies.

I can get used to optimism like that rubbing off on me, even if it's packaged in a guy with a love of Jesus fish.

7

• • • • •

Black Gold – Soul Asylum

I follow Stephen's car, reaching Bishop's Peak around noon, the sun heavy and beaming. We meet up with his friends, Delilah and Howard, bespectacled with matching high-waisted khaki shorts and Christian Youth T-shirts depicting a bunch of stick figures holding hands around a spinning globe. When I step out, each greets me with a hug and cups the back of my head. Hella Awkward.

"This is Nico," Stephen says. "We met at Pismo. She wants to see the top of Bishop's Peak."

"Are those your hiking boots?" Delilah asks. I can tell she wants to frown at my busted Doc Martin's, but she seems incapable of doing anything but smiling.

"I'll manage."

"You can turn an ankle," Howard says, and gives Delilah a grave look.

"I'm indestructible."

I find out that the three of them have known each other since they were little kids in Sunday school. They have in-jokes just like Winter, Jeremy and I, except all their in-jokes center around Jesus as a punch line.

Don't judge, don't judge, don't judge, I tell myself and strain to smile through my inevitable sarcasm. Stephen is super cute, and San Luis Obispo seems like a chill enough place to stick around for a while.

I sling my Jansport over my shoulders. There isn't much in it besides my Walkman, notebook, and a couple of joints should this Christian party start to go south. I also have my Polaroid camera.

"Could you take a picture of Stephen and me?" I ask Delilah. "Let's have the mountain in the backdrop."

Stephen puts his arm around me and I nuzzle in close. He gives a peace sign so I do the same as Delilah snaps the pic. Stephen whips out a pen as we watch it develop and then writes on the back, The glory of a beautiful picture to always remember this day by! Stephen, 805-555-9879, 1818 W. Foothill Blvd, San Luis Obispo 93401

Howard gets out the trail guide, telling us precisely the route we'd take so we could make it back before it turns too dark. I have a feeling he'll get on my nerves soon enough.

We begin hiking along the left side of a wooden fence, leading to a wide dirt trail that passes through a shaded oak forest.

"So Nico caught a wave for the first time," Stephen says. He rolls up his sleeves around his shoulders, perspiration lining around his thin muscles.

"Bless," is all Delilah and Howard say in response. I'll have to figure out a way to get Stephen alone and drop these two lame-o's. But then I think of Stephen's words, how he waited until someone's actions revealed who they were rather than making a snap judgment. I swear to try to give the Jesus kids more of a chance.

We follow a wide road up a grassy slope and pass through a cattle gate that leads to a junction with a connector trail, heading farther up the grass skirt of Bishop's Peak. So far, we aren't high enough yet for me to really freak out. I hope I won't lose my shit in front of Stephen.

"So, tell us more about yourself," Delilah says. She'd snuck up behind me, ninja-like. She has box stitch lanyards on her wrists like a little girl and wears a retainer. She smells of the Jean Nate I used to wear when I was nine. Her wide eyes are creepily expressive.

"I'm doing a road trip from L.A."

"On your own?" Howard asks, with a little bit of a judgmental tone.

"Uh-huh, just me and my car."

"Where did you stay last night?" Howard asks. Now I'm bookended by the two of them.

"In my car at the beach."

Their eyes lock on one another.

"Do you have a home?" Delilah asks, shimmying up extra close.

"Of course I have a fucking home."

The three of them stop in place. Delilah withdraws and shuffles over to Howard who has his hand out to rub her back.

"Nico, we're not about cursing," Stephen says. He isn't smiling.

"Curses are words designed to hurt others," Delilah says.

"I didn't curse," I reply.

"You did," Howard chides. "It started with an F."

"Oh yeah." I wave off their accusations. "Fuck isn't a curse, it's just an expression. Like, my friends Winter and Jeremy and I say it all the time. It has so many meanings and is truly a lovely word."

"I'm going to ask you not to say it around us," Stephen says. "If that's okay. We're all about freedom of expression, but we want this hike to remain pure."

If he weren't so cute in the way he asked, I would've bolted back to my car right there.

"Okay," I say, slapping my forehead in mock-embarrassment. "It'll be a good test for me."

"There is no testimony without a test," Delilah says, pushing her large glasses back up her nose.

"Ri-ght," I reply. "I'll keep that in mind."

We continue on, weaving through a shaded forest. The three of them begin singing a religious song that repeats the same God-lovin'-verse over and over ad nauseam. I hum along to show I'm a good sport. We switch up to a rocky sun-exposed trail along the mountain, the hike becoming strenuous. I look back to see that we're getting rather high up.

"Oh shit," I murmur, as Howard and Delilah cut me with their eyes. "Really? Shit's a curse too?"

"Are you okay, Nico?" Stephen asks. He's so nice. He can tell that I'm scared about something. I want him to carry me up the mountainside like a bride and then lay me down on the rocky soil so we could make out under the clouds and I could feel his Jesus schlong grow.

"Yeah, I'm a little afraid of heights." I look back

and see that the trees below appear so small. "Okay, a lot afraid."

"Here, look at me instead." Stephen takes my hand and then directs my face so we're staring at each other. He gives me his winning smile.

Howard and Delilah cross their arms, tapping their feet in annoyance. Some patient Christians, I want to say. Isn't patience a virtue?

"Why don't you guys go ahead while I help Nico out?" Stephen says to them, and I nod in response.

"The point of this trip is for the three of us to reach the top together," Delilah whines.

"A bigger point is to help those who need it," Stephen says, reminding her of the difference between actual goodness and a fake ass bitch.

"All right, we'll take a break a little while up and meet you then," Howard says. He and Delilah swivel around and are gone.

"I'm sorry I'm holding you back," I say.

"I don't see it in that way. Every experience is a worthwhile one."

"You have such an optimistic outlook about things."

"Imagine if more people did. There'd be less anguish, less hatred I imagine."

"You have a great smile too. It, like, beams."

He chuckles. "Yeah, I've gotten that before. I should do tooth commercials."

"Can I hold your hand?" I ask. "I think that would make me feel more secure as we climb higher."

"Sure." He takes my hand, his grip strong. If someone passed by us, they'd assume we're boyfriend and girlfriend alone on a hike. I like the power of that thought.

"So, you're not into religion much, are you, Nico?"

"I didn't mean to make your friends think I'm some degenerate sinner."

"Part of our youth org is about finding other teens who might need us. Howard and Delilah are always on the lookout."

"Thanks, but I'm good. Like, my grandmother was super religious and raised my dad and my aunt that way. She died a few years back, but she, like, gave all her money to the church and spent all her time there. It was weird."

"Why is that weird?"

"For her, everything was about God. Every conversation directed back toward Him. It was exhausting to be around her."

"Well, God is everywhere."

"Okay, but there are other things to focus on in life too."

"Of course, there is and I do. Like surfing. I sing in a choir too. But God is with me while I do all that, looking out, making me feel special. Do you have that?"

"No... I mean, I have close friends to rely on."

"Where are they now? Back in L.A., right? See for me, wherever I go, Jesus is there as my buddy. Doesn't that sound nice?"

"Yeah, I like my space. Don't you ever want privacy?"

"You really are funny, Nico. Of course, I have privacy and Jesus always respects that. He doesn't come into the shower with me."

"I never took him to be a perv."

"But no matter what, he's still inside of me. The

world is a very scary place so it's comforting to think I always have someone with me throughout my journey."

"My Aunt Carly says that the older we get, the more people come and go."

"Except for Jesus," he says, tapping me on the nose. I feel myself blush. We are still holding hands. I turn around and see we've climbed a ton more, completely forgetting about being afraid of heights.

"You aren't thinking of how far up we are, are you?" he asks.

"No," I gush. "You make me feel really safe. Can we rest for a sec?"

"Okay."

We find an orange boulder to sit on surrounded by a thriving brush. Before us, the green hills and valleys are lush and vibrant; the kind of view that tells me anything is attainable. Stephen licks off the sweat from his top lip, and I wish I were the one to do it for him instead. I inch closer until our shoulders are touching.

"It's so pretty, isn't it?" I ask, just to make conversation. He nods, his Adam's apple bobbing up and down as he swallows. "Kind of sets the mood, doesn't it?"

He turns to me, the moment about to happen—a boy I actually liked. Not just one I found attractive while I was high out of my gourd. A true connection. And even though I'm not super down with his Jesus speak, some of what he says makes sense. It's sorta nice to think of someone with you all the time, like how I'd begun to imagine Kristen with me, another soul along this crazy journey.

"Nico..."

I kiss him in response, his eyes bulging. He recoils

back and I could immediately feel his distance, his lips receding far away.

"Sorry I…"

"No, I'm sorry, Stephen." I throw my head in my hands. "I like you, and just with the view, the moment felt right."

"I like you, too."

"Oh good," I say, my lips reaching out for more.

"But, I don't just kiss girls. In fact, I only kissed a girl once before, and I want to really save it for my wife."

"Your what?"

"The girl I'd truly fall in love with. I'd want all my firsts to be with her. Storybook, kind of. But I'm only seventeen. It's not something I need to happen now."

"So you've never slept with someone before?"

"No. That would be for my wedding night."

Ugh. Just my luck. I meet a pretty awesome guy who's a stone-cold virgin. No Jesus schlong for me.

"Is that okay, Nico? I don't want you to think I'm rejecting you. You're very beautiful."

"You don't have to say that."

"No, you really are. Don't you see it?"

"I'm about twenty pounds overweight."

He cocks his head to one side. "No way! I mean, do you really think that? You're tiny."

"Tiny for a beast. Look at my thighs!"

I point to my fatty evidence.

"I really don't see that. If you lost even ten pounds, you'd look emaciated. When is the last time you weighed yourself?"

"Yeah, I don't do that."

"You're perfect."

"Why because God made me that way?"

"No, because you are. You probably have to fight off most guys."

I blow a raspberry. "Not really. I'm strange and misshapen."

"That's all in your head. I don't know, maybe when you were younger you felt that way so it stuck. But please don't think of yourself like that anymore. And I don't lie, God's honest truth. I was very upfront with you about myself so you should believe what I say."

"That's true."

"Any guy would be lucky to have you. Don't sell yourself short. But I'm just not built like that, so I can't kiss you again. Please understand."

"I'm sorry I lunged at you like you were a piece of meat."

"I'm flattered." He puts his arm around me as a good friend would. "Come on, let's catch up with Howard and Delilah."

• • •

We reach the top of Bishop Peak with a spacious view of volcanic rocks leading out to Morro Bay. Howard and Delilah are already there, spreading out a blanket and cutting up Italian bread and cheese to make sandwiches. I'm a little shaky on my feet still, but Stephen hasn't let go of my hand, and I feel better once I sit down. I still might go tumbling to my death, but the sights are really freakin' amazing. The day is clear, so I snap another picture while the sun remains high in the sky.

"See, that wasn't so scary," Stephen says. We join Howard and Delilah for cheese sandwiches that we shovel down our gullets like we haven't eaten in days.

"You should come to our event tonight," Howard says, watching me carefully.

"What is it?" I mumble, spraying breadcrumbs.

"It's for lost souls," Delilah says, twitching her nose like she is Queen of knowing every-goddamn-thing.

"I'm not lost," I say, and want to continue with, And I will cut a bitch.

"You're homeless, Nico," Howard sighs as if I'm a burden. "You live in your car, you haven't showered, and wear ratty clothes."

I throw my sandwich to the ground. "My clothes are purposely ratty, it's a grunge-look. Didn't Jesus dress in rags anyway?"

"You don't have to respond with sarcasm all the time," Delilah says. "We'll save your darkened soul."

"Are you hearing this?" I ask, looking toward Stephen for help.

"You should think about coming tonight," is all he says.

"Really? You think I'm a lost soul, too?"

"Delilah didn't describe it right. It's for everyone who needs some...assistance."

"I'm not homeless!" I scream, the echoes passing along the land. "Do you actually think I don't have a home?"

"You're sleeping on the beach."

"I'm on a road trip."

"You're a runaway," Howard says, with contempt, like I'm Tonya Harding or someone terrible like that.

"So what?" I kick at the dirt by my feet. "Maybe I did run away, but I come from a good home." I couldn't believe I was defending my parents of all crappy people, but I don't want these morons to think I'd been abused or kept locked in an attic or something. "I live in Laurel Canyon. My dad makes a lot of money in finance."

"Money doesn't buy happiness," Delilah adds.

"Is everything you say a stupid cliché?"

"There's hatred in your heart, Nico."

"There's hatred in this fist," I say, holding it up. "Wanna taste of it?"

Delilah scurries her butt closer to Howard.

"Your friends really are shits," I say to Stephen. I hear Delilah gasp.

"Nico, there's no need for that," he replies.

"Was all of this engineered to save me?" I ask, as hot and angry tears start to build.

"You did seem like you could use a friend when I saw you on the beach."

"Yeah, a friend, not a conversion!"

I jump to my feet, wobbling at first as the steepness swirls around me.

"Whoa," I say, getting my bearings. Stephen reaches out to grab me, but I swat him away. "My sister fucking died okay and my parents are divorcing, so I…I don't know, I just took off. I want an adventure."

"I'm so sorry about your sister," Stephen says. He reaches out again, and I want to spit on his hand.

"Save it. You all preach that you're so above everyone else because of your closeness with God, but you are the biggest judgmental pricks out there.

I'm outta here."

"Nico," Stephen says, trying one last time to console me by reaching out. "This isn't what we intended."

"God, screw a girl, you virgin pussy. Live a little."

It's the first time his smile really fades, and I can tell that I hurt him. Good. I wish I could take back that desperate kiss we had. I sling my backpack over my shoulder and hike my way down as I hear Howard and Delilah telling Stephen to "let me go." I feel him rush up behind me.

"Nico, please don't leave like this," he says, out of breath.

I swing around and clock him in the arm, harder than I mean to. He stumbles back, gobsmacked by what I'd done. He rubs his developing bruise.

"No one's ever hit me before," he says, his lip trembling.

"Maybe it is about time then," I snap. "What does Jesus think of that?"

"It makes him sad."

"Oh God," I yell, rolling my eyes. He's still calling out to me, so I pop in my headphones as Soul Asylum's "Black Gold" comes up.

"This side's yours, that's side's mine," I shout back at Stephen, singing along to the lyrics. "Brother, you ain't a friend of mine." What am I doing with a God boy anyway? This has been even more of a deluded mistake than my chronic dalliance with Gregg with three g's. I'm the opposite of pure. Stephen and his two friends had judged me from the jump as a homeless heathen, so that's obviously the persona I convey. It pisses me off that I even let Stephen into my heart a little—the last time I'd ever do that. Nico versus the world is how I have to be for the rest of this trip. Not trusting anyone, an army of one. I wipe away any wimpy tears I cried for Stephen; he deserves none of my sorrow. And even though one of my bucket list items is to kiss a boy I really like, I need to stop making dudes the center of everything. That's what dumb girls do, go gaga over guys who don't even give two shits. One thing about me is—I definitely ain't dumb.

When I reach my car, I slam on the gas and shoot out of San Luis Obispo as fast as I can, its three Jesus-worshipping denizens eating my goddamn dust.

8

• • • • •

Daughter – Pearl Jam

I make it back into town, dying for a drink of some kind. I'd already lit one joint out of the window and suck until it's just a nub. I spy a liquor store and figure I can either try with my fake ID or just swipe a bottle. Screw it, I figure, time for some kleptomania on this trip. The guy behind the counter is watching the news covering the Menendez Brothers trials, which has captivated my mom and the rest of the nation. She's a sucker for all things sordid, switching away from soap operas that suddenly had less appeal. Since I'm a pro at thieving, I already have my bag unzippered and go right for the wine section, longing for a sleepy, emotional kind of drunk. I eye the dude at the counter who's still transfixed with the TV, make my selection, and slide a twenty-dollar bottle into my backpack. He doesn't even glance over as I pass through the electric eye to my freedom outside.

To avoid getting picked up for public intoxication, I head back into my car, untwist the cap, and chug,

chug, chug. The wine runs hot down my throat, the acid making my lips pucker, my belly gurgling. On the seat beside me rests the picture of Stephen and me with Bishop's Peak as a backdrop. I can't believe how much of a disaster that bucket list item turned out to be. Do I really look like such a mess that people could mistake me for homeless? I glance in the rearview mirror to see a girl with bloodshot eyes and fried blond hair the color of egg yolks. Yuck. I need to remedy that. I put down the bottle for a second and drive a few blocks down to a gas station. After parking the car, I remove some lavender Manic Panic hair dye from my duffel bag, grab the bottle of wine again and make my way into the gas station bathroom.

Plugging up the piss smell wafting into my nostrils, I pour the lavender dye over my struggling hair and then chug more wine as I wait for it to seep in good. In the mirror, I lift my Soundgarden T-shirt to stare at my midsection. Stephen had said that I'm not fat and if I lost weight I'd look emaciated, but it was probably just part of his strategy to get me to trust his Jesus ass. I go to pinch my midsection, expecting to grab onto some major tummy, but in all honesty, there isn't really that much to squeeze. When I was younger, I did look chubby and maybe I still carry around that insecurity. Body-wise I don't appear to be that bad. Decent tits. A long and quite elegant neck. Not a completely flat stomach, but it isn't out of the realm of possibilities if I do some exercise. I bring the wine bottle to my mouth and gulp until there's nothing left. That'd be enough exercise for now.

I dunk my head under the faucet and let a hot

stream pass over my face. With a paper towel, I dab my brand-new hair, satisfied with my kick-ass color. I march outside and see a phone booth, swaying over and slipping quarter after quarter inside. I find myself dialing my home number and I'm about to hang up when Mom answers.

"Hello?"

"Did I catch you at a bad time?" I ask, slurring. "Is Mr. Ferguson on top of you?"

"Nico?"

She doesn't seem too excited to hear my voice. Maybe in my few days' absence, she's already grown accustomed to not having me around. Her life a little easier without Hurricane Nico mucking it all up.

"Yeah, it's Nico, your only daughter. Remember her?"

Mom doesn't answer right away, probably thinking about Kristen because of what I said. But I don't feel bad. I'm drunk enough to seep like a puddle down a drain. And I'm thinking about Kristen too. How her stupid runaway of a sister couldn't even run away right.

"How are things at Winter's?" Mom asks. She hasn't mentioned the school contacting her so Winter must've had Edina take care of that. Edina is a good mom.

"It's amazing," I shout. "Edina is hella cool. We go for hikes in the mornings and drink smoothies and listen to sixties records and she's teaching me how to sew."

I don't know where these lies are coming from, but they sound convincing. I grin at the thought of Mom being jealous.

"I never knew you wanted to learn to sew."

"There's a lot about me you have no clue about."

"Nico, I know you're angry–"

"I don't care who you're porking, Mom–"

"About your father and I splitting up. He's not here right now. He's moved to Los Feliz. I'll leave the number with Winter's mother."

"You can do whatever the hell you want, I don't care."

"We weren't there for you," she says, quietly.

"What?"

"When Kristen died… You can't know what it's like to lose a child."

"And you can't know what it's like to lose a sister."

My throat is dry, my tongue like sandpaper. Tears attach to my cheeks refusing to let go.

"It isn't about who's hurting more. We need to learn how to heal together."

Mom is starting to sound worse than the Jesus kids.

"Nico, why don't you come home? We shouldn't be having this conversation on the phone."

"You had about a million chances to talk to me while I was there, but you were always so distracted."

"That's how I managed to cope. I love you, Nico."

I hang up the phone by slamming the receiver. I don't want excuses. I'm not sure what I want, but certainly not any desperate attempts to make herself feel better. She's the parent and I'm the child. I should get the focus.

I picture her still on the line trying to tell me she loved me again, only to realize I'm not there anymore. I know she won't try to call Winter's house to talk to me again for a while. This fight would give me a few days off without having to contact her. And if she calls Edina to give her my dad's number, there's no chance I'll reach out to him either.

I wander back to my car and slam on the horn as I let out a scream. In the rearview, Kristen emerges. She wears her Umbro shorts and a baggy off-the-shoulder sweatshirt with her high school's name. She isn't happy how I'd spoken to Mom. She makes that clear with her presence.

"I'm a terrible daughter," I say, lighting another joint. "I know."

"You have to give Mom and Dad a chance again sometime," Kristen says, always taking their side. It was usually like that, the three of them versus me riding solo. At least it seemed to be that way.

"And I'm not letting you drive, Nico."

She joins me in the front seat and takes the keys out of the ignition.

"What are you doing? I need to get out of stupid San Luis Obispo."

Kristen rolls down the window and dangles the keys outside.

"I'll throw them away."

"I can drive."

"You can go to sleep now, that's about all you can do."

She plucks the joint from my fingers too.

"Come," she says, directing me to her lap. "Lay your head down."

My chin quivers as I listen, the only person right now whose advice I'd take. She strokes my hair as I lie down.

"I like the purple, brings out your eyes."

"You'd hate the color if you were alive, I know you would."

"Maybe I've changed since then."

"I'm trying to change too," I say, blowing a tearful spit-bubble that hangs on my lips.

"I know you are. You just faced one of your biggest fears by climbing that mountain."

"Yeah, but the rest of that experience turned out shitty."

"So what? God, Nico, I remember going with you to Big Sur when we were nine or ten and you screamed bloody murder the whole time. You had to wait at the bottom with one of the counselors."

"But I have that great picture of you and I there."

"Yeah, that was right when we arrived before you went insane."

"I didn't go insane."

"Memory can be a fickle thing. We choose what we want to remember. So forget everything else about today and remember it as the day you made that mountain your bitch."

I smile. "I did make it my bitch."

"Sssshhh, bedtime for Nico."

She turns on her mixtape as "Daughter" by Pearl Jam pumps from the speakers at a low volume. She sings the words into my ear, a fuzzy lullaby that eases me into dreamland.

• • •

I dream of a Halloween night long before I lost Kristen. We were probably about ten and eleven and she'd dressed up as a teen mom and I was her baby. We'd bought adult diapers from CVS that I wore, and she'd gotten candy cigarettes that she pretended to smoke. With the amount of hairspray in her hair, she probably killed a thousand trees. We went trick or treating from house to house in Laurel Canyon and had to explain our costumes to everyone who opened their door. Most threw candies into our bags with revulsion, offended by the spectacle.

"This is my daughter," Kristen would say. "I had her in the gym locker room after prom. Isn't she the cutest baby ever?" Back then she had more of a sense of humor.

"Do your parents know you've dressed up like this?" someone asked, turning up their nose at us.

"These aren't costumes," I yelled, removing a pacifier from my mouth. "It's the late eighties. We're in modern times and my mom is the best teen mom out there so get used to it!"

The typical response after this was a few Bit-O-Honeys tossed in our bags followed by a door slam.

"People can't take a good joke," I remembered saying, as we walked hand-in-hand back home.

"My baby daughter is growing up so fast," Kristen said, kissing me on the cheek. "I just love her so."

That was probably the last Halloween we spent together. When Kristen went into seventh grade, she started her new private school and had a zillion new friends to hang out with rather than me. Turning eleven was also when I met Winter and the two of us drifted away from everyone else: wearing only black, piercing each other's ears and bleeding over one of Edina's pashminas, even beginning to skip school. Two little terrors on a mission to hell. Even though Kristen's room was just across the hall, it began to feel like a planet light-years away. By the time the next Halloween rolled around, Winter and I dressed up as Madonna from "Like a Prayer" with papier-mâché crosses taped to our backs. When I went to show Kristen, she had already left for her own party with a bunch of girls on her track and field team.

"I can take a picture so we can show your sister," Winter said, her dozens of bracelets jangling as she reached for the Polaroid camera.

"Nah, she won't care. We barely hang out anymore."

"I'm your sister now!" Winter screeched. She slid out a pack of cigarettes from the cleavage she was already sporting at eleven.

"Those are real cigarettes!"

"Duh, Nico." She passed me one and whipped out a lighter too. She lit mine and I inhaled, coughing like mad. "Coughing is good, means your lungs are getting used to it."

As Winter and I left, I spied the picture of Kristen and me as a teen mother and daughter from the year before tacked up to the corkboard. I crumpled it up and tossed it in the trash.

What I'd give to still have that picture.

I have so few others of us together.

9

• • • • •

Hunger Strike – Temple of the Dog

After sobering up by the morning, I drive up the 101 to San Francisco. I want to blend into anonymity there: go to coffee shops, listen to bands, write some lyrics, get my shit together. But I've heard about the beauty of Muir Woods and figure I'll try a peaceful walk through its forests. My expeditions in Ojai and San Luis Obispo had been focused on guys too much. Here I'd gone to the top of a freaking mountain and it hardly registered because I was zeroing in on Stephen's Jesus schlong. So far, I've barely spent any time with myself, my thoughts, my reflections. Muir Woods could be my wake-up call. So I stuff the picture of Stephen and me in my pocket as a firm reminder not to be stupid over a boy again.

I buy a guidebook that says the Redwoods here are the tallest living things in the world, the height of a six-foot person stacked head-to-toe forty-five times. Pretty freakin' cool. The oldest one is over a thousand, each tree playing a significant role in carbon, nutrient, and water cycling in the forest. One of the items on my bucket list is to give back to nature in some form. I used to be really passionate about the environment after doing a paper in eighth grade about the horrors of acid rain. Winter, Jeremy, and I even once protested outside of our school; but no one seemed to care.

It's a wet and moist kind of day having rained during the night. I know about San Francisco's weather and how you should always carry an umbrella. So far, the sun still finds its way through the gaps in the trees, and it probably wouldn't be worth it to go grab the umbrella I left in the car. While walking, I remember reading Walden in tenth grade English class. Our teacher Mr. Henrickson made us go to a park every day so we could read Thoreau under a tree. It was kinda corny but eventually pretty cool. There'd be moments when I'd forget about whatever had been pissing me off and I just got lost in the words. Most subjects I barely paid attention to, but English I actually liked. While books don't have the same appeal as music, ones like Walden I can dig. Besides, living in a zoo like L.A., it can be hard to find moments of calm. One of its quotes always stood out: "I have, as it are, my own sun and moon and stars, and a little world all to myself." Such a feeling could never happen while honking at each other on a freeway, but walking through Muir Woods, the pot and alcohol seeping out of my pores into the cool air, there's no one else around except for me, the champion and queen of my own destiny.

A little way into the woods, a group of people surrounds a Redwood. Coming closer, I see they're chained to the massive tree. A few police officers mill about along with some reporters taking pictures. Some kind of protest or demonstration. I don't want to talk to a cop, I'm still hesitant due to when the officer showed up about Kristen and the fact that I'm also a runaway. Some lady is writing about the goings-on in her notepad so I ask her.

"They call themselves Treeactivists," she says. I couldn't tell if they impressed her or not. "Do this from time to time. Chain themselves up and refuse to eat trying to stop deforestation."

"Is this tree being cut down?"

"No, but protesting in Muir Woods certainly gets people noticing."

"How long have they been here?"

"Since last night. And anyone can join them. They've even got a few new members this morning."

The Treeactivists consist of about a dozen people ranging from an old grandma to a guy who looks to be my age with his hair in a ponytail and Birkenstocks on his feet. They chant slogans like: "We won't eat until our forests are safe," "Deforestation destroys," and "Hug a tree, don't kill one." The few cops tasked with this assignment look bored, the reporters barely more engaged.

The grandma zeroes in on me. "An estimated eighteen million acres of forest are lost each year, that's the size of Panama."

"That's terrible."

"About half the world's tropical forests have also been cleared," Grandma shouts, spittle flying from her lips.

"That's terrible too."

"Well then, help us protest, little girl." She raises her fist that isn't chained to the sky. "We'll stay here another night if need be. I don't have to eat for days."

I've just massacred a McDonald's breakfast burrito that's settling nicely, so I can probably go for the rest of the day without eating too.

"Where can I chain myself?" I ask.

Grandma indicates either a spot by her or the guy with the ponytail. I go to attach myself next to him, but then think twice. I remember my promise not to make this journey about dudes anymore. If I chain up next to him, he'd distract me, I'd do something ridiculous to make him realize what a craptastic person I am, and then the whole cycle would start up all again. So I choose to go in between Grandma and another lady who didn't seem too jazzed to have me there.

"Are you serious about this?" she asks. "We don't want any lightweights."

"Oh, I've protested a ton before. The last time was against acid rain."

As the day progresses, the Treeactivists gather an even bigger audience. Evidently the ponytail guy's father runs the show, a man named Milo who wears John Lennon glasses and looks like a duplicate of his son aged twenty years. He's the most vocal of everyone. He calls the police "pigs," and says anyone who watches but doesn't participate is just as responsible for destroying nature as if they chopped down the trees themselves. Grandma echoes everything he says, and then turns to me with a look that says, "You see, Milo means business." I don't know how long we've been protesting, but I imagine it's probably about time for lunch.

"How long has it been?" I ask Grandma. The other lady, whose name is Raquel, answers instead.

"We have been here for about twenty hours now." Her nostrils flare. "You have been here about two."

"What do you do if you have to use the bathroom?"

Raquel rolls her eyes. Grandma answers this one.

"You go right in your shorts. I already did. Warms ya up."

"Fantastic," I say, smiling through a grimace.

I tell myself to see this through no matter what. Every other item on my bucket list so far has been a selfish one and sacrifices like this would only make me into a better person. Someone more like Kristen and less of a hot mess. So instead of Raquel, I picture Kristen chained beside me. She'd honestly be so proud of me for doing this. She used to do all kinds of volunteer work and try to tell me how privileged we were and how I had to give back, but I never wanted to hear it. Volunteering would cut into my music listening/pot consuming time; therefore I deemed it impossible.

I look over at Grandma. Doesn't her back hurt? Mine's already starting to act up. I let the Jansport slide off my shoulders, then I reach in and grab my Walkman, fast-forwarding until I find Temple of the Dog's "Hunger Strike." I let Chris Cornell's shrill pipes take over the forest until I can see Grandma indicating for me to take out the headphones.

"What?"

"No, darling," she chides. "How can you be vocal

with music in your head?"

She starts chanting again so I put the Walkman away and mimic what she's saying. While it feels good to be doing something other than for just myself, I have the desire to unchain, smoke a jay, and wander through the woods before it gets too dark to do so. I feel a drop of rain splash on my head and wonder how much the forests are really worth saving if I'm about to get drenched?

"No!" I hear Kristen's voice whisper. Her eyes are steely, focused. I'm her only concern.

"You need to see this through," she says. "Remember when you protested against acid rain. You were so enraged when you found out that the government was barely doing anything to stop it. And so you protested and got detention."

"Ugh, it was so boring in detention with Mrs. Willicker who always had lipstick on her teeth and would shush us right in our face."

"But I was proud of you because you stood up for something you believed in."

Her voice sounds harmonious, jingling through the tall trees.

"I didn't even know you knew."

"You had more balls than me. I was angry about acid rain too, but I'd never risk detention."

"I do have big balls."

"Melon-sized." She smiles, something I rarely saw her do. Dead Kristen seems more alive than when she actually was alive, her nose no longer glued to a textbook.

We're protesting together, sisters against the establishment. Rock fucking on.

"Now stick this out," she says. "Okay?"

"Okay," I tell the trees, shifting in place so I can get a more comfortable stance.

• • •

Once nighttime hits, the rain luckily lets up, but the Treeactivists are shouting even louder than before while my spirit is starting to dim despite Kristen's words o' wisdom. Okay, I'm really hungry, I have to pee, and I'm not gonna wet myself like Grandma. The park's commission arrives and we're all threatened to either leave or be arrested. My ears perk up at this. While it'd be badass to get arrested, a night in a cell after a day standing in the woods doesn't sound like such a great experience.

"None of us are leaving!" Milo shouts, to cheers around him.

Raquel gives me a look that clearly tells me I'd be spat on if I chicken out. I'd made it through a few hours already so I can't give up now. Grandma's eyes start to close.

"Are you okay?" I ask her.

"I've been on my feet for twenty-four hours."

She'd meant to say it as an act to be respected, but it sounded more like she's in disbelief.

"Maybe you should eat something?" I whisper. "I have granola in my backpack."

"Pshaw," she says. "Does a raped tree get a chance to eat?"

"Huh?"

"Why are you even here?"

One of her twitching eyes zeroes in on me like before.

"I want to help the environment," I say. "Give back to nature."

"Did you read that on a bumper sticker?"

Grandma is beginning to piss me off.

"No."

"You have nothing better to do, that's the real reason." She massages her arm chained to the tree, wincing at the soreness. "This means everything to me. What do you really care about? And don't say, acid rain."

"I care about music."

She nods, as if she accepts my response. "So why aren't you doing that right now?"

I have no answer to that. I don't say anything, hoping she'd get the hint.

"I used to love the swing and big band music of the forties. Used to dance all night."

"I'm into grunge."

"Don't know what the hell that is," she says, frowning.

I wonder how to describe grunge music to someone who's never heard of it before. I take this as a challenge.

"Grunge is, like, the subgenre of alternative rock and a subculture that emerged in Seattle in the mid-eighties."

"I don't know what the heck that even means."

"It fuses elements of punk and heavy metal like the distorted electric guitar and the lyrics are about alienation, confinement, and a desire for freedom."

I'm happy with my wordy description, but Grandma shakes her head.

"Sounds like a bunch of nonsense to me."

"It isn't, you old bag."

"So this crazy music you like so much?" she asks, shrugging her thin shoulders. "What do you want to do with it?"

"I want to fucking sing."

"So sing, you whiny brat, what's stopping you?"

I start to reply but the screeching of police sirens driving up the road towards us stop me. My fellow Treeactivists start chanting louder as men in blue descend upon our tree. They clip off chains as I watch people fight against being handcuffed. Milo is thrown to the ground, a cop's knee shoved in his back. His ponytailed son gets tossed into a police van. A reporter snaps a picture and the flashbulb remains in my vision, distorting the scene. Grandma licks her lips as if she's just eaten a delicious pie when the cops unchain her and slap on handcuffs.

When they come for me, I buck like a horse trying to throw off its rider, screaming about my rights, the passion heavy in my voice. I'm dragged to the van.

"My bag, my bag!" I yell, because it holds Kristen's mixtape, my last piece of her.

"C'mon," the police officer snaps at me.

"But my backpack, it's important!"

"The forests are what's important!" Raquel says, while she's being carried past me.

"Kristen," I mumble, tasting tears. I'm lifted into the van as the doors shut and I can still see my red Jansport, alone by the tree, possibly separated from me forever. Someone else would eventually find the mixtape, but it'll have no meaning for them—a string of unconnected songs, not a way to show a sister how much she meant.

The van speeds away. As the trees whip by on our way out of Muir Woods, I hate every goddamn one, wishing them all to be torn down.

10

• • • • •

Falling to Pieces – Faith No More

We are all thrown in a holding cell. Apparently, this isn't the first time the Treeactivists have been locked up, the sheriff's station is getting tired of their misconduct. While they seem to wear it as a badge, I'm freaking out over Kristen's mixtape I'd left behind in Muir Woods. I ask the cop outside of the cell multiple times if he can tell me whether they had the Jansport, and he always answers the same way.

"Sure, kid, lemme take a break from policing murderers and rapists so I can locate your stupid backpack."

"But there's something very important in it!"

I also just realize I've left my pot in the front zipper. Whoopsie. He dunks a donut into his coffee as a response.

"Selfish," I hear, and glance over at Raquel who's far from a fan of mine. "This is bigger than you right here and all you can worry about is a backpack?"

"Take a chill pill," I say. When I turn around,

she's right in my face.

"You never cared about our cause. I smelled that about you the minute you joined our chain."

Ponytail Guy directs her away from me, which is good since I'm about to pop her.

"Don't mind, Raquel," he says. "She's just passionate."

"Or certifiable."

"I heard that, Purple Hair," Raquel calls out from the other side of the cell.

"Usually they just keep us overnight," he says. "But since this is our third offense, bail is gonna be steeper."

"Bail?" I haven't even thought about that, trying to decide who I'd call. The 'rents are out of the question. Aunt Carly is probably on her way to being wine wasted already tonight, Winter and Jeremy stoned out of their skulls too—none of them able to drive for four hours.

I have the sad realization that everyone I'm close to is an even bigger basket case than me. I root around in my pocket and pull out the picture of Stephen and me, his phone number on the back. Calling him for help would be a true test to see how much of a good Christian he really is.

"That your boyfriend?" Ponytail asks.

"No, just part of a long list of mistakes."

"You're very intense," he says, as his father Milo comes over.

"Starr, you haven't introduced me to your friend," Milo says.

I try to mask a laugh. "Your name is Starr?"

"My son's name is beautiful," Milo says. His

graying beard coils around his face like puffs of smoke. He smells worse than me, probably not even remembering his last shower. His back hair spills out from the top of his T-shirt and even more hair flows from his nose and ears.

"Sure, it's beautiful," I say, sarcastically. "I'm Nico."

The holding cell is drafty and bugs collect around our one barred window. A sad toilet in the back has already overflowed and warns us all not to sit. I'm freezing wearing just jean shorts, a Screaming Trees tee, and a red and black flannel.

"Nico," Milo begins, giving me a phony grin. "We would prefer it if you stay silent for the rest of our time in jail. You've already bothered the cop."

"You were calling the cops 'pigs' earlier!"

"That was in the heat of the moment, certainly not how I feel now." His voice rises as he talks in the hopes that our cop might hear.

"My sister's mixtape is in that backpack. You don't understand how much I need it."

"Are you really carrying on about a damn mixtape?" Raquel yells.

"The Treeactivists aim to change the world," Milo says. "We have many other demonstrations lined up this week and therefore can't stay in here."

"I got plans too."

"Meaning the more you agitate, the greater chance that they'll keep us."

"My sister died," I say, making eye contact with everyone in the cell. "And that mixtape is the last thing I have of hers."

I wait for their pity, but they all stay silent.

"She had a brain aneurysm and dropped dead on a run last Halloween!"

I pause so their sympathy can flood in: a hug, at least a pat on the back. Nothing.

"Do any of you tree fuckers even care?"

"Language!" Grandma snaps, plugging up her ears, my one possible ally turning on me.

I'm getting tired of everyone censoring my cursing. People really need to take all those giant sticks out of their asses.

A different cop enters the hallway leading to our cell and waltzes over. I'm practically trampled with pleas from the Treeactivists to be let out.

"Shaddup, shaddup," he says. "You can all make your one call."

I'm led to a room that has a yellow rotary phone. The fight I'd just gotten in rattled me. How could people who love nature be so uncaring? Previously, every time I'd mention my sister dying, I'd get a flurry of consoling, even if it's unwanted. How could they be so cold as to not give a shit? But then I wonder about all the people who might have lost someone and how I never thought much about them and what they're going through. Like even Mom and Dad who pop up in my mind when I don't want them there. While losing a sister sucks, losing your kid—God that must just be awful. I start to feel bad about how I hung up on Mom when she was trying to vent her feelings. And Dad? Even an ice block like him has to be shattered inside. I hoped his French lady is helping him heal because his only daughter certainly hasn't made an attempt.

"So, who you gonna call?" the copper asks. For a second, I consider one of the 'rents but then this bucket list run-away adventure would be over in a flash. So I get out the Polaroid of Stephen again, take a deep breath, and dial. A few rings pass before someone finally answers.

"Is this Stephen?"

"Yeah," a sleepy voice says. "It's really late. Who is this?"

"It's Nico."

The silence scrapes at the air. I expect him to hang up.

"Are you okay, Nico?" he asks, completely not what I'm expecting him to say.

"No." I release a flood of tears. "I'm in jail. I...had no one else to call."

"A jail in San Luis Obispo?"

"No, San Francisco. I need to be bailed out."

I wince, really expecting him to hang up now. But people can surprise you. Goodness exists in this toilet tank of a world.

After a long, winded breath, Stephen replies: "Give me all the details and I'll come and get you."

• • •

While I'm waiting for Stephen, I ignore the Treeactivists' complaints and go over some new lyrics in my head. I do this whenever I want to tune out the world. I don't have a pen but I'm able to imagine well.

If you haunt me for the rest of my life

Is it just as good as if you were
actually here?
Or will it never be enough, my floating
Kelly ghost?

Stephen finally shows, and I've never been so excited to see a God boy before. I give the middle finger to all the tree-lovin' haters and skip out of the holding cell. I'm proud of myself for standing up for a cause even when it was difficult. For once, I did something that didn't benefit just moi. Once I'm let out, I'm not sure whether to hug Stephen or shake his hand. His eyes are tired, his back hunched, hair uncombed. It must've been about three in the morning.

"Are you okay?" he asks.

Screw it, I think, hugging him anyway, my nose against his neck. "I can't believe you came."

"You need help."

I ignore his concern. "How did your parents even let you go to San Francisco in the middle of the night?"

"I told them the truth and they encouraged me to go. You said you had no one else."

"My parents would've shit a brick."

The donut cop comes over with a Ziploc bag. "Here's your stuff," he says. "You're free to go."

He hands me my wallet and car keys, but there's no mixtape.

"Wait, this can't be it! I had a backpack."

He shakes his fat index finger. "No backpack."

"It must still be in Muir Woods." I grab Stephen's hand. "C'mon!"

Now I'm super freaked out. Someone had to have

taken it, since the world is full of super sketchoids. I yank sleepy Stephen to his car, explaining to him about the mixtape, and how my car's left at Muir Woods anyway. He nods, but I can tell he's probably regretting coming all the way here for my ass.

Because of how late it is, we're the only car on the road. I have no clue what to say to him. If the tables were reversed, I would've likely just hung up.

"Thank you so much, Stephen," I say, gnawing at a glitter-painted fingernail. "How much do I owe you for the bail?"

"It's okay," he replies, but clearly it isn't.

"I have my dad's gas card. Can I at least get you back for the gas?"

He lets out a sigh full of disappointment that makes me feel so low.

"This will be on your record now, you know? Arrests don't go away."

"It was for a good cause! We were protesting against trees being cut down."

Here I go and do something awesomely unselfish and I still get shit for it.

"You're just trying to push the envelope, Nico. It's not a good look."

"Don't all sixteen-year-olds try to push the envelope?"

I'm acting cute, satisfied with my witty retort. When he doesn't respond, I turn on the radio searching for an alternative rock station and find Faith No More's "Falling to Pieces." I crank it up and give myself devil's horns as I thrash.

"It's too loud," Stephen says, but I'm grooving to

the music and don't care. "Nico, it's too loud."

He snaps it off, fuming. It seems like he wants to be anywhere but here so why the hell did he even come? I certainly don't need his disdain and he's starting to way piss me off. I feel the blood coloring my cheeks.

"Look, I'm sorry I dragged you out of bed to come and save me. Sorry, sorry, sorry, okay? But if you did it because you think I actually had a chance at being saved, you're so fucking wrong."

He pinches the bridge of his nose while keeping one hand on the wheel. "Could you not curse?"

"Fuck, shit, damn, bitch, tit, orgy, asshole, schlong."

"Nico, things aren't going to end well for you. You're ready for a crash."

He gulps when he says this, a scary oracle. But I salivate at the thought of this crash, delicious and freeing. The medicine ball of sadness that's heavy in my stomach would finally be removed. The fear of dying always more frightening than the actual act. I drop my voice to a sultry whisper like Jessica Rabbit's.

"If you think I wanna crash so bad, then take your goddamn foot off of the accelerator and let's let God decide what happens next."

He looks at me like I'm crazy, veering oh-so-close to insanity. Little does he know that I'm a nutso and sick of being stuck in my diseased mind. I always pretend that everything is everyone else's fault but my own. Deep down I truly hate myself for that, but I have no clue how to be any other way. And I don't see that changing anytime soon.

"Did you really come help me so I could be your next saved victim, Stephen?" I ask, steering the conversation away from myself.

"If this is your rock bottom, then I want to show you there's a light..."

"Enough!" I put my hand up in his face. Then I turn back on the radio, cranking up "Falling to Pieces" until the song shakes the car. I sing along because my voice is loud enough to be drowned out. Stephen shuts up, smartly realizing these are demons I have to release and that music can give me the best exorcism possible.

• • •

We reach Muir Woods by dawn, the sun breaking hot and misty over the horizon looking like a pathway to heaven if you believe that kind of thing. I'd kept the music blasting all the way and Stephen allowed it through gritted teeth. Finally, I calmed down.

"I'm nervous if the backpack's gone," I say. "I feel like that mixtape is all I have that still connects me to Kristen."

Stephen slows the car down to a stop. "What you've been through is terrible."

I sniff up a snot ball. "Thank you. Like, everyone I was protesting with didn't even care that my sister died."

"But she can't be your excuse for behaving the way you do."

He's so wrong since I behaved just as terribly before she was gone. It's my nature, in my blood to be wild, my true parents were wolves. I slam my arm into the door and fly out of his car, stomping up ahead. I can hear him shuffling behind me.

"I don't need any more lectures," I howl to the trees.

"Let's just call it a day. I'll find my backpack on my own. You're free to go."

He tugs at my flannel, stopping me from continuing.

"I don't know what it's like to lose a sister." When I swivel around, his eyes are watering. "Mine is twelve, she's just a child. The thought of her dead..."

Great, now I have to console him.

"She's not gonna die."

"You thought that about yours."

"My grandfather died the same way, it's something in our family. Which means I'm probably going to be gone soon too."

"Is that why you act the way you do?"

I'm too exhausted from a night without sleep to stay angry, too tired to even keep my guard up, my impenetrable stone fortress.

"I don't know. Like, I'm always angry. Even more-so now. I see people and they're smiling these big stupid smiles and I want to, like, rip that smile off their face cause no one is that happy. Everyone is so fake. You probably love everyone."

"We're supposed to love everyone."

I suck in a cold hit of air. "I don't even love myself most of the time."

I bite my lip, surprised to hear those words. I've thought it before, sitting on the roof of my house, California tucked in a puff of smog. The sensation of rushing toward the ground below, my brain cracked on the asphalt.

"That really hurts me to hear," he says, pulling me away from that horrible vision. "You're special, Nico, we're all special. Think about when you were conceived and all the millions of other hopeful lives that didn't make it."

"That's so weird, dude," I say, trying to laugh everything off like I always do.

"Every second, every breath...is magical. And we should give thanks for our creation."

"Well, what was the point of my creation? What have I done that's so meaningful? I just take up air and space."

"I heard you sing when we were in the car."

"So?"

"While the song was not my cup of tea, you have an amazing voice. One touched by God, I'd say."

"You're just trying to make me feel better."

"Will you sing for me?"

"No. I don't like really singing in front of people."

He swept his arms out. "No one's around, it's like, six in the morning. Only nature's listening."

I begin to walk away. "I want to find that mixtape, Stephen."

"You owe me," he says, his smile beaming, teeth pearly white. "And while I won't accept a payment in cash, I will take a song, Nico."

"Will it shut you up if I do?"

He crosses his chest. "Swear to it. How about that song from on the radio, but not screaming like that singer. Can you make it acoustic?"

"All right, bossy. I only do this for guys who bail me out of jail."

I clear my throat and take a deep breath, the woodsy air circling up my nostrils. I close my eyes until everything vanishes. I can't look at him, since I've never truly sung in front of anyone before without the radio as an accouterment. What if I miss a note or my voice cracks? What if I'm not as good as I think I am? I decide that Stephen is a nice enough guy even if I don't have chops, and therefore, the best possible person to practice on. So I give the Faith No More song a mellow Mazzy Star kind of spin, my tone quiet and melancholic.

I leave my body for a while, knowing the song well enough for it to breathe on its own. I'm a songbird soaring through the clouds. I have no worries, only the music exists, with the fragments of my tattered soul. I give them to Stephen, to Muir Woods. It's the only gifts I have. The end is whispered to Kristen, a warning that while I'm still falling to pieces, she's assisting me in slowly fitting them back together. I take a sharp breath as the song ends, my body lighter, a balloon untethered in the sky.

Clapping echoes in my eardrums as I open my eyes, transported back onto land.

Stephen stands there with a gaping grin.

"See how special you are, Nico? I don't think these woods has ever heard a concert like that."

I can barely catch my breath, my heart sounding like a chainsaw rumble. I'd gone somewhere and got sucked back altered, hopefully for good. I'm buzzing like the happiest bee in the land.

"You're so talented! I mean, you really are. Pipes like an angel."

"Yeah, yeah," I say, waving him off and looking away. "You're really a great guy, God boy."

Stephen points to the sky. "I'll tell Him you think so. Come, let's get your mixtape."

• • •

Sure enough, my Jansport is lying against the Redwood. I burst out of the car and unzip it to find my yellow Walkman with the mixtape stopped at "Hunger Strike" as I'd left it. I hug it close to my chest and glance up at the sky.

"Thank you," I say, to all who are listening and guiding me.

We drive back to where my car had been parked. I finger the buttons on the Walkman.

"Ya-know, you really saved me, Stephen. Please let me mail you the money."

He shakes his head. "Do something selfless for someone else, then you've paid me back."

"You're too good for this world. Can I hug you?"

"Of course."

I wrap my arms around his neck, squeezing his thin body close. I've got an urge to kiss him again like before but know that I have to squash that. My out-of-control libido needs to be put to rest. Stephen's meant to meet a girl so they could adopt a million starving babies and travel the world from Peace Corp to Peace Corp. I'd only sully him.

He pulls away but looks carefully into my eyes.

"Please take good care of yourself. Don't crash."

"I'm putting on the breaks." I mime the motion.

"When in doubt ask yourself, What Would Stephen Do? I guarantee that'll show you the right way."

"You're such a dork."

He kisses me on the cheek and takes off a black and gold friendship bracelet made of hemp. He ties it around my wrist.

"You always have a friend in me, Nico. Even when things are at their worst."

"I think I'm better now," I softly say, seeing a bird hovering overhead and knowing that I'd just returned from touching the clouds too.

"I hope so, but if you find yourself in another jam, I'll always pick up the phone." He smiles his tooth commercial smile. "Good luck on the rest of your bucket list quest."

He dashes into his car, looking like he was about to get choked up. While I've never met someone like him before, I bet he'd never come across a tornado like Nico and his life would be a little less exciting without me.

I wave as his car pulls away. When it's a tiny dot ready to disappear into the atmosphere, I get back in my own. I flirt with lighting a joint after my stressful last day but decide I don't need it at the moment. I take out my camera and snap a photo of the majestic nature that helped unlock my voice.

I'm content with the sun spilling over my windshield as it lights the road ahead. So I drive straight into its welcoming rays, eager for whatever I'd encounter next.

11

• • • • •

Miss World – Hole

While I'm hella jealous of Courtney Love because of who she gets to lie next to every night, Hole's music actually rocks. As I drive, I sing "Miss World" until my throat is red, knowing I should support female musicians that are part of the Riot Grrrl movement rather than tear them down. The scene came out of Olympia where women could express themselves in the same way that men always did. Bands like Bikini Kill, Bratmobile, and Heaven's to Betsy, a DIY ethic with zines, political activism, and Sassy mag dealt with tough subjects aimed at teen girls like me. Being from L.A., I felt removed from the scene, my glossy sun-exposed life at war with the moody, rain-soaked Pacific Northwest. But I'm angry like they are. I want to have a voice too. Courtney Love is the most recognizable one attached to feminist punk. L.A. girls who feel like they're outcasts at school wore her crooked tiaras and smudged their eyeliner. They ripped their fishnets, rarely washed their hair (guilty as well), and made a statement with their defiance. Winter, Jeremy, and I thought they were all lame. We don't want to be attached to any grouping. We want to love the bands we're devoted to and find meaning in the music that we don't have in our actual lives. We're lonely and neglected. We simply want to be heard by those who could relate to our alienation.

Winter says she'd go lez for Courtney Love, mostly because she believes Courtney has access to her other crushes that'd make it worthwhile. It has been a long time since I talked to her so when the song ends, I park the car and trap myself inside of a phone booth, inserting a zillion quarters.

"Hola," comes a voice on the other line, high-pitched but not Winter's.

"Jeremy?"

"Nico Nicotine?" he squeals. "Nico Rico Suave?"

"That's me."

"Girl, what is going on? How's the runaway going? Somewhere in Timbuktu by now?"

"It's good–"

"So here's the dope news from back home. I kissed a boy! Yes, bitch. A real boy, not a blow-up doll. Do you know Asa Levenweld?"

"I don't think so."

"He's a sophomore. Punky. Dyed green hair the color of nuclear waste. Nose ring. Anyway, the other day he is all, do you wanna smoke after school? I'm like, yesssss, and I had good stuff. We were in the park and no one was around because I was like, we have to find a secluded spot. I took a puff and then he asked if I wanted to shotgun!"

For those with no clue about shotgunning: one

person takes a hit of pot and holds the smoke in their mouth. Then they press their lips onto someone else's mouth and open their own while the other person sucks the smoke in.

"Girl, I saw all the colors of the rainbow when we did it. Like, we fucking made the fuck out."

"That's great Jeremy," I say, wrapping the heavy phone cord around my finger. I'm eager to talk about what I've been doing, but also happy to hear him be so excited. I think of Stephen saying to do something unselfish for someone else and repeat over and over in my mind to not interrupt Jeremy when he's so pumped about a boy. He's certainly listened to Winter and I yammering on about the same thing.

"We have a meet-up again at the end of the week. This time I'm aiming for tongue."

"Get that tongue."

Jeremy squeals and I hear him toss the phone across the room.

"Jer, you almost broke it," Winter's muffled voice says before getting on the line. "Looks like you got the play-by-play. I've only heard it about a thousand times."

"And you're gonna hear it a thousand more!" Jeremy yells.

"Jeremy, go make some Totinos pizza rolls so Nico and I can talk."

"Pepperoni, bitch!" I hear him say, followed by the sound of the door slam.

"He's high as a pole vaulter right now and getting on my final nerve," Winter says.

"Think about when you had your first kiss."

"I was, like, seven. I don't even remember. I don't

even remember my first dicking. Is that bad? Anyway, what's new with you?"

"I was arrested."

"Give me all the deets."

"It's not that exciting. I was protesting against trees and the cops took us in. But this guy I met in San Luis Obispo came all the way up to San Fran to bail me out."

"Oooohhhh, so gallant. What's he like?"

"He loves Jesus, volunteers in a youth organization, and won't hook up with a girl until they marry."

"I fully dried up from that description. Ugh."

"No, he was great. Like, how many genuinely nice people do you ever get to meet?"

"None because nice equals boring."

"Maybe boring isn't the worst thing."

"So are you gonna marry his Christ-loving wang?"

"No, he just made me realize...it's hard to put into words."

I think about when I became a songbird as "Falling to Pieces" emerged from my throat for Stephen and all of Muir Woods. I'd been so against singing in front of someone (other than when I was too messed up to notice) that I'd talked myself into remaining silent. But that's just stupid. Stephen was definitely not a liar and said my voice needed to be heard. So I'd really do it eventually. For me. For Kristen who never got to pursue her own dreams.

"Oh shit," Winter says. "I forgot, your dad has been calling here non-stop. Every time I made an excuse that you're in the bathroom. He fully thought you had Montezuma's Revenge until I lied and said that you are just constantly dyeing your hair."

"I recently dyed it lavender by the way."

"Hot, mine is still ghost-white."

"That's my Winter."

"Anyway, his new number is 323-555-8741. Call his ass so he leaves mine alone."

"Thanks again, Wint."

"You sound good. More like the old Nico, the one I fell in love with."

I pause for a moment wondering if that's true, but I can feel her inside, scratching at the walls of my body to fully break through again.

"Yeah...maybe I am getting back to her."

"Aces. Okay, gotta go. The pizza rolls are ready."

She hangs up. I get back the change leftover and dial Dad, hoping his French paramour won't be the one who answers.

"Hello?"

"Dad?"

"Nico? Listen, when I call you, I expect you to drop what you're doing and answer."

Uh-oh, Dad is already not messing around.

"Dad, if I'm dyeing my hair, I'll get it all over the phone."

"I refuse to leave a message with that space case you're staying with. Has she told you anything that I said?"

"Uhh...."

"I'm settled in Los Feliz at Annette's. You'd like her. She has a pool."

"Whoopee, I hate to swim in chlorine."

I fall right back into the only relationship I have

with Dad, trading sarcasm like pros.

"I want you to come out to dinner with us so you can meet her. It's getting serious."

"Serious, like, you've knocked her up?"

"Why do you have to be so crude all the time? Is that really how I raised you?"

Did you really raise me? I want to ask. Turning out the hallway light when you'd come home at midnight and peeking into my room was barely raising me.

"Look Dad, I'm me, you're you. We're a different species."

"So does that mean you have no interest in meeting Annette?"

"Not right now. Can you give me some time?"

"Sure." Sarcasm ruled his tone too, the biggest gene I'd inherited. "Take all you need, Nico. How's my gas card doing by the way?"

"Er...I gotta go, Winter made pizza rolls."

If he ever actually checks the purchases I made so far, he'll see I'm a long way from Edina's house.

"What?"

"I'll meet Annette soon, Dad, okay? Don't have a titty attack about it."

"I can't understand half the things you say."

"Likewise, parental unit."

The phone clicks, meaning my time is about to end. We mumble "good-bye" to one another, both of us likely glad to be free. He'd done his duty by checking in with me. I'd done my duty by making him believe I'm at Winter's.

I step outside, longing for a coffee shop, a bar, or a band playing a show. I'm ready to get back to scribbling lyrics in my composition book. Two punk girls pass by.

"Hey!" I say and am met with two scowls. "Sorry to bother you...I'm not from here. What's a good place to hear a band?"

They both look me up and down, not nearly as punk as they are since I don't have a safety pin through my earlobe.

"What kind of music you into?" the one with the bigger safety pin asks.

"Nirvana...so something like that."

The smaller safety pin, points to a lamppost filled with flyers. "Nirvana cover band plays tonight at Blitzen's. We would go but we have something way cooler to do."

They cackle as they head away. I stick up both of my middle fingers. But one of the flyers does advertise a Nirvana cover band called Drain You playing at Blitzen's. Show starts at eight and it's six o' clock now. Enough time to find a gas station and use Dad's card to get myself another soggy hot dog that has become my dinner for the last few heartburn-filled nights in a row.

• • •

Blitzen's is a typical dive-bar except for the atypical stuffed reindeers hung up on the walls. The opening band is playing when I get there, easily making it past the bouncer with my fake Sasha Lioni ID that never does me wrong. The openers had a Hole vibe, three chicks in torn dresses skuzzing out over rioting wails. They called themselves Cobain's Pharmacist. I order a

Long Island Iced Tea at the bar because it's the kind of drink where you get the most alcohol for your dough. A mosh pit has started up so I knock back the Long Island and dive in, jabbing my elbows in spleens and getting a bruise on my right tit. When the band stops playing, I'm sweaty and spent, blood dripping from my lip, my flannel lost in the pit, scratches down my arms. I go to the bar and get a Bud this time. I look over at the guy sitting on the adjacent stool. Messy blond hair covering his eyes. Butt chin. Deep-set eyes. Face scruff. A heavy sweater too big for his frame.

"Holy shit, are you...?" I start to ask, afraid my head will explode.

"I'm not Kurt Cobain," he says, sucking the hell out of a final hit of a cigarette and incinerating it into the ashtray. "But thank you, I'll take it as a compliment."

"You must get that all the time," I say, taking a swig of cold beer.

"Comes with the territory of being in a cover band."

"You're in Drain You?"

"You a fan?"

"Gotta admit I hadn't heard of you before. I'm from L.A. But I'm stoked to see you play."

"Kurt," he says, extending his hand as I give him a screwy look. "That's really my first name."

"Nico," I say, wanting to bite his lip. I'm swooning big time so I tell my libido to calm the hell down. It's only brought me anguish so far and I'd made a promise to swear off dudes for the rest of this jaunt. Also he looks to be about thirty, and the two of us together would be illegal.

"So, Nico from L.A., what brings you to Frisco?"

"I'm on a road trip up to Seattle, actually to see your house."

"You think I'll let you inside?"

"Not if your wife has anything to say about it."

"Ah Courtney, Nancy to my Sid."

"Didn't end so great for them."

"Don't think it's gonna be any different for me." He soars his hand through the air and then crashes it into the bar. "What goes up, must come down."

I feel a chill in my bones, an ominous presence lurking. Death around the corner. I've had this sensation before, usually when Kristen sneaks into my thoughts, embalmed like a cadaver instead of just a ghost. But she isn't there this time.

"Your music makes me want to live," I say, unable to control the words from spewing. He pops a cigarette between his lips and nods in response as if I'm just a crazy fan who's gotten too close. I blink and X's cover his eyes, his tongue lolling out of his mouth. I picture us on a chugging train headed for a collision.

"Excuse me, I need to get ready to play," Kurt says.

He spins off the stool and is gone, his cigarette smoke hanging behind as a reminder. I down my beer and welcome another, unnerved by what has just occurred. I take out my Polaroid and snap of picture of him up on stage that's sure to be blurry, since I took it so quickly.

Kurt leaps up on stage with his two other bandmates, launching into "About a Girl" off of Bleach; his mournful moans a dead ringer for Cobain's. A mosh pit takes over the area in front of me, but I don't want to join this time. "Serve the Servants" comes next with its jarring opening blast, followed by "Heart-Shaped Box" with its dramatic guitars and gloom, followed by "Lithium" with its soft and loud bipolar temper tantrum. Next up is "Breed" with its aggressive sway, and then "In Bloom" and its morose harmonies, ending with the passion and violent cries of "Smells Like Teen Spirit," which leaves me weeping because I have an eerie premonition that I'd make it to Cobain's house but he wouldn't be there anymore. All that remains would be a memory of what was and a nail in the coffin of the grunge music I'd worshipped so much.

Drain You ends with a few Hole songs afterward, a surprise. During "Miss World" it seems like Kurt is singing it right to me, even though probably everyone at Blitzen's is experiencing the same funk, longing for an idol to meet our gaze and uplift our sorrows. But is Cobain really any different from any of us? I imagine him alone in his room, struggling to write lyrics, spitting at the fame that crawls up his walls. We've all been bruised in our own ways; death and success intertwined for some. I want to run to him and tell him to hang on because I've decided to hang on. I won't wind up in a grave next to my sister, at least not for another seventy years, and he should stay strong too.

I bolt out of Blitzen's into the cool and moist night, finding my car and curling up into a ball in the backseat, ready to finally leave California in the morning and penetrate the Pacific Northwest so I can give my man the advice he needs to not do something drastic and break a million hearts in the process.

12

• • • • •

Crucify – Tori Amos

I didn't sleep well last night because twice a cop knocked on my window and told me to wake up and move my car. Like anyone else was looking for a spot at three or four in the morning. The second time it happened I took it as a sign to get the hell out of San Francisco already. The morning starts off gloomy, the clouds flirting with launching a downpour. I find the drawing Aunt Carly made for me of the sunrise in Ojai and tape it up to the passenger's side window. Therefore, even if the weather appears miserable, I can look over and see the sun.

Sure enough, the weather worsens along the drive up I-5 North. Torrential rains rock my car, the windshield wipers barely doing their job. Even my mixtape can't uplift my mood, but maybe because I've hit the Tori Amos section of the tape, which is downright moody. I try to have some conversations with Kristen to pass the time, neither of us knowing what to say.

"You think I'm beginning to do better?" I ask,

nibbling on a fingernail and spitting the remains out of the window. "Like, was this runaway a good idea?"

"I guess."

Has Kristen become bored with me already like she did when she was alive and gave zero fucks about anything that excited me? Am I being selfish by making her hang out in this purgatory when there's possibly some cooler place she should wind up permanently—like staying in heaven? I want to talk about singing in Muir Woods and how it made me feel, but it doesn't seem like she's game right now. She appears so sad, her mouth dangling into a permanent frown. Maybe singing for the first time in front of some dude wasn't enough to warrant her interest. What more does she want?

Her ghost had been a surprise addition to the trip at first, now it's simply awkward, which super bums me out. We've retreated to the relationship we had, two sisters who couldn't be more different in their likes and dislikes. So I let her vanish for the time being and my thoughts float to the strange conversation I had with Kurt from Drain You. He'd said Cobain's time is limited, a pilot light about to go out. The idea of that chilling beyond belief. A shiver rocks my bones.

Around noon, after eight hours of driving, I hit Eugene, Oregon and decide I can't see straight anymore. I don't crave a drink or smoke, I want a fancy coffee filled with loads of sugar and to sit in a coffee shop and listen to music while getting a burst of lyrical inspiration for the rest of the day.

Eugene is a sleepy little city surrounded by mountains and the greenest trees I'd ever seen. Hippies roam the streets and even the adults dress down, the weather and climate a likely explanation. I spy a parking spot by a coffee shop called Café Hey with a sign for open mic spoken word and song.

Inside smells of scented candles, the décor full of old furniture and couches you could sink into. I order a chai latte and plunk myself down, whipping out my notepad and plugging in my headphones. The place isn't super crowded at this hour. It takes a second to remember what day it is and I realize it's a Tuesday, most people are in school or at work. The University of Oregon is close by so the few people scattered around look to be college students. A dude with long curly hair on a comfy-looking chair vaguely reminds me of Gregg with three g's. Two punk guys, their skateboards propped up against the nearby couch have eyebrow piercings and shirts and jeans three sizes too big.

I look over the lyrics I'd already written on this trip for "Nico's Lament."

Spiral to vanish
Ebb of the tide flows strong
Dark beneath the blue
Ice between my toes
Circling fishes give up hope
If you haunt me for the rest of my life
Is it just as good as if you were actually here?
Or will it never be enough, my floating Kelly ghost?

I'm realizing that while Kristen's ghost was novel at first, now it's only making me more aware of her absence. A flood of sadness quivers through my body. I grip my pink pen tight.

What I wouldn't give to see your real smile
Not just your see-through doppelganger's
She's a poor imitation
And I've been living in a twisted fantasy

I shut the composition book, choking back a sob. God, I'd been doing so well only to spiral again. Maybe this is what my life would be, an ebb and flow of depression. I dig my fingernail into the skin of my arm until a dab of blood emerges and I feel kinda better. Pain to topple other pain. I've cut before, but never really, only as a test. I shake away the sensation of digging in deeper and flip the pages to my written bucket list, goals I shouldn't let out of my sights. I'd done a good number already, but still had a lot of the real ones to complete.

Nico's Supa Fly Bucket List

Learn Guitar

~~Climb a High Mountain and Get Over My Fear of Heights~~

~~Sleep Under the Stars in the Wilderness~~

~~Go Surfing~~

See Seattle and the Real Grunge Scene

~~Give Back to Nature in Some Form~~

Kiss a Boy I REALLY Like
Go to Kurt Cobain's House
Push Aside Courtney Love And Maul My Hero
Get Front Row Seats to Nirvana in Concert
Sing In Front of a Real Audience (not just in the shower)

What would Stephen do? I whisper, realizing he'd search for the good things I had left to accomplish and wade away from this swell of misery. So I vow to take a swim to that brightened shore and plaster a shit-eating grin on my face that would scare away tiny children until it manages to settle into something normal looking.

A girl across from me wears old lady librarian glasses. She has pinkish-red hair and a skull cap, a checkered flannel that goes down to her knees, frayed jeans shorts over black stockings, red nails to match her lips, and the Nirvana T-shirt with a smiley face and X's over the eyes. My kind of girl.

I sip my latte as Tori Amos croons in my ears and start sketching the girl across from me with my average doodles. She looks like she's doing some kind of homework, headphones in her ears as well, silently nodding to the beats. I try to think of a way to start a conversation with her. With a guy, it's easy. If a dude looks at you like you're a piece of meat, I know they actually want me. But how to get a girl's attention? I think about current events I could bring up. The Tonya Harding and Nancy Kerrigan scandal, for which I'm controversially in Tonya's corner since Nancy Kerrigan comes off like a whiny brat. Who wouldn't club her ass? Lorena Bobbitt had just been convicted for chopping off her husband's penis, and I figure he'd probably deserved it since guys could be such dicks. Haha, pun intended. Sweet, I think, I'm already making jokes again. The Menendez Brothers are obviously guilty so there isn't much to talk about there. We could discuss the World Trade Center bombing, but that was over a year ago and the fear everyone felt from it already old news. Of course, Bill Clinton and his sexy jogging with a hamburger in hand is always a good option. A grunge girl like her definitely wouldn't have been sad that George Bush only lasted one term. But no, I need a wowza opening for a girl as cool as her.

"I like your glasses," I say. Her music plays loud and she doesn't hear. "I said I like your glasses."

The two skater guys look over and then whisper something to each other, either about her or me.

"I'm sorry, did you say something?" she asks, pulling aside one headphone.

"Your glasses are rad."

Wow, I sounded ten years old. She gives a half-smile, one that told me she doesn't want to be mean and not smile at all.

"I need to get glasses soon so I'm always on the lookout for cool styles."

This is an outright lie, but I needed to say something else to salvage the conversation.

She takes off the glasses and hangs them around her neck, attached by a string.

"These are my grandmother's. I'm really into old

fashions mixed with new ones."

"Me too!" I say, although this is another lie. I have zero dated clothes in my closet back at home.

"You at U. of Oregon?" she asks.

I debate whether to lie and morph into Sasha Lioni, but unlike Gregg with three g's I don't want this girl for a fuck and run. I'm missing Winter and Jeremy and longing for a new friend, any friend right now.

"I'm in high school," I whisper.

She looks at her watch and finally gives a full smile. "Playing hooky?"

"Major hooky. I'm from L.A."

"What are you doing here?"

I point at her Nirvana shirt. "Taking a road trip to his house."

She looks down. "Cobain's?"

"The one and only."

She pats the seat next to her. "Come on over."

Her name is Lacey. She's a poetry major and manages a band. She grew up nearby, at one time thinking she'd venture out of Oregon, but never gelling with people as much she did with other Oregonians.

"I love our laid-back attitude, but at the same time we're so passionate about causes and the environment," she says.

"I just came from getting arrested in Muir Woods for protesting against deforestation."

She gives me a high-five. "Wow, Nico, I wish I was like you at sixteen. I mean, that was only two years ago, but I never had cojones like you. I want to make a change, but... I dunno, I never do anything major."

"I don't give a F, I guess."

"No, that's awesome. Usually L.A. girls are so self-centered, no offense. L.A. has this glossy sheen to it like nothing there is real. Is that why you want to get away?"

"There are lots of reasons. Family shit being the biggest."

"I hear you. Part of why I'm going to UO is because my parents wouldn't pay for my school and at least the tuition is low due to being in state. They're very blue-collar and don't believe in education."

"Mine would go ballistic if I didn't continue onto college."

"They don't sound half-bad then."

I give her a screwy look. "I guess everyone thinks their parents are the worst."

She makes a gun with her thumb and index finger and shoots me.

"So, Cobain's house?" she asks. "What are you gonna say if he opens the door?"

"I think he's getting out of rehab. But I just want to see it. Like, where greatness sleeps."

"Favorite Nirvana songs?"

"I love "Drain You." And "Polly" and "Pennyroyal Tea" and "Silver" and "All Apologies." Of course "In Bloom"."

"'In Bloom' is my favorite," Lacey says. "I love how the guitar in the song's chorus is so heavily layered. It's quiet, then loud, quiet, then loud."

"Totally. I just saw a cover band in San Fran that played it well."

"Ever actually seen Nirvana?"

"No."

"I have. It was, like, a religious experience." Her eyes light up thinking back to the memory. "It was in Portland about a year ago. Cobain played so hard his fingers bled. They were celebrating the release of In Utero, which they said was the record they truly wanted to make, stripped of production and fucking sublime."

"Yeah, it's on my bucket list to see them before I die," I say, my voice becoming quieter, my lips quivering. I'd forgotten for a minute about my sad destiny—the creeping brain aneurysm—only to be thrust back into reality.

"You okay?"

Crap, my eyes are starting to water. Kristen's ghost glides through Café Hey's doors and orders an espresso. She's watching out for me, not ready to give up and I'm glad to see her, even if it's not real.

"I'm sorry," I say, as a few tears drip into my latte. "My sister just died, and I...I don't know how to deal sometimes."

"Oh man," Lacey says, shaking her head. She hugs me, not out of pity but because she understands. I can feel the pain in her heart beating against mine.

"My sister had an overdose," she says, wiping her nose. "Like, she wasn't a druggie or anything. Just curious. And this guy she was dating gave her some heroin."

"I'm sorry, Lacey."

"It was about five years ago, but sometimes I'll wake up in the morning and for, like, two seconds, I'll forget. I'll want to her tell her about the dream I had, or a date I went on, and... Look at us, two sniveling depressives."

"That's why I'm running away to Seattle. I'm doing every item on my bucket list."

"Very inspiring," she says. "What's the number one thing you haven't done yet?"

"Well..."

"C'mon, Nico," she says, poking me in the spleen. We grin through our tears, both exhausted from crying. How much salty water can one body hold? "Tell me, however gnarly it might be."

"It's not gnarly, I'm just...afraid. Okay, I want to sing in front of an audience. Like, a real audience. I've always wanted to be a singer."

"Voila," Lacey says, sweeping her left arm out and directing my sight toward a stage and a sign that says Open Mic Tonight.

"No way," I say, the reality of actually doing it bursting through the door.

"Yes way! We'll come back tonight, and you'll do it." She claps her hands. "If you don't, you'll never forgive yourself."

"I choke up when I'm in front of people," I say, totally wanting to do it but so afraid, the worst scaredy-cat on the planet.

"So what if you choke? It's an open mic in a coffee shop, no one is expecting genius. But if you're amazing, they might remember."

"And if I blow chunks all over the stage?"

"Then sleepy Eugene has a story for the ages. C'mon, let's go to this thrift store a few blocks away and plan your outfit."

"My cash is limited."

"It's on me. Please, let me do this." She clasps her fingers together, genuinely excited. I can't believe someone I just met cares so much. "I love a makeover. Let me turn you into the roaring chanteuse you deserve to be."

Kristen's ghost sits at the counter and gives a sharp nod, confirming this decision. Maybe this will be what gets her excited again so she can lose her frown. Her visits have been engineered to remove my crippling fears. I can't let her down.

I feel like I have to poop, my organs spinning around, but Lacey is right that I'd regret it if I don't finally sing my heart out.

At least I'll have one person in my cheering corner section, and it seems like Lacey could cheer loud enough to get a crowd on her side.

• • •

"You need more accessories," Lacey says, as we roam the aisles in the thrift shop. "Like, make a noisy presence when you get up on stage."

She chooses a ribbon choker with various silver necklaces dangling from it that attach at the back of my neck. For bracelets, she brings me bangles. Instead of a band T-shirt, she gets me a crop top, since evidently, I have nice athletic boobs. The checkered flannel I'm wearing can stay, and we find a pair of frayed jeans with holes around the knees and thighs. For make-up, she gives me a pale glow with red lips, red blush and a red hue around the eyes for a wan and healthy strung-out look. The outfit is finished with a hat that resembles the one the 4 Non Blondes singer wears.

"You look like Drew Barrymore!" she says, as we observe my new look in a bathroom mirror.

"No, she's so much prettier."

"Nico, you're a fox. Do you really not see that? I'd do you."

We laugh at that.

"Lemme take a picture of you. You have a camera on you?"

"Sure do," I say, and hand it over.

I give a pose with a peace sign as the flash causes floaties. She hands me the developing picture.

"Ready to open up those pipes?" Lacey asks.

For a second, I think she is being weirdly sexual but then realize she means my vocal cords.

"No, but I can't back out now."

When we return to Café Hey, it's way more crowded than earlier. Obviously, it's a popular spot to hang in the area. Students overflow off the couches. Lacey sees a few of her friends that she introduces me to.

"Nico's gonna sing tonight," she tells them.

"I've never sung in front of an audience before," I admit to the floor.

"Time for a cherry pop," her friend Clarissa says while making a popping sound with her finger on the inside of her cheek.

I sign my name up for the open mic, sweating a storm as I wait through others going before me. I can't even listen to their poems or songs, too nervous to think about anything else but my own performance. I decide to go with Tori Amos because I'd been listening to her the most recently and I definitely know all the words. As much as I love Nirvana, my voice is very different from Cobain's, and I'm not sure it will sound good.

"And next up, Nico Sullivan," I hear the MC say, as we make eye contact and he waves me up on stage.

I look out at a crowd of about twenty-five people, every finger in the room pointing at me. My fat thighs. My hat that's trying too hard. My growling stomach. My shaking knees. All of them waiting to crucify.

"Woo hoo!" Lacey shouts. "Go, Nico."

I grin at her support because it causes a few other people to clap as well.

Taking a deep breath, I put my lips against the microphone and close my eyes. I retreat to my own private café, only Kristen as an audience.

"Let me hear you sing, sister," Kristen says, raising her fist in solidarity. She's smiling again, the sad frown extinguished.

I open my mouth as Tori Amos' "Silent All These Years" escapes after being stuffed down for so fucking long.

13

• • • • • •

Silent All These Years – Tori Amos

I'm silent at first, the lyrics tucked deep down struggling to break free but they're blocked and I'm shit scared that they'll never make it out of my body. I worry about barfing an Exorcist-like spew of all the hot dogs I'd eaten over the last few days. Or crapping myself, or getting my period at that exact moment, or forgetting the English language and just making baby noises. But I have a gift and it's wrong to keep it hidden. The first words slip out in a throaty vibrato along with the piano accompaniment, and I'm damn proud of myself. Café Hey disappears, and it's just me and Kristen. She's swaying to Tori Amos, a singer she actually never hated. She whips out a lighter and I focus on her eyes twinkling in the low light. I'm taken back to a time when we were little and I had a nightmare about a monster in the attic named the Big Bad so I crawled into her bed instead of my parents'. She was listening to a Walkman playing Belinda Carlisle's "Heaven is a Place on Earth." We stretched out the headphones, tiny head against tiny head, so we both could listen. The tears slowed down and I thought that heaven on Earth was right there in Kristen's bed as she stroked my cheek and whispered the lyrics until morning magically came and the Big Bad got obliterated.

I'm moving along on the stage to Tori Amos, acting out the song and making the words believable. I'm floating high above Café Hey and can see my performance and a rapt audience. They don't expect this grungy girl to have pipes, but I know I'm delivering it because Kristen's eyes have grown wide and are brimming with tears. Her hands are clasped together as if she's praying for me to do well and my heart is swimming, electrified from this imagined fantasy finally coming to life. I monitor my breathing so I don't get winded and can properly sing the powerful conclusion loud enough for Kristen's ghost to take it back with her all the way to heaven.

When I finish, it's quiet for a second. I wonder if the entire thing has been in my head and I just stood there without giving a show. But then the applause starts along with shouts and hollers, not just from Lacey but also from the entire audience at Café Hey. People are whistling; a girl up front even has tears staining her cheeks. Woah. The applause won't cease, caressing me with adoration, touching me all over. I need to find my center of balance, worried I might topple over.

The MC leaps up on stage and takes my hand, which is sweating so much it nearly slides out of his grasp.

"Nico Sullivan everyone." He's shaking his head. "That was phenomenal."

"Really?"

"Look at the crowd."

I turn and see everyone has jumped to their feet. I hide my face in my hands and peer through an opening between two fingers. They won't let up! They want more! I'd rocked everyone's world.

"I think it's a good time for a break," the MC says, to the crowd. "Remember to tip your barista well."

I make my way over to Lacey who's leaping up and down.

"Nico, I'm stunned." She hugs me close and I'm vibrating. "Like your voice has such a beautiful sadness to it. And you have such a presence. You owned that stage! There's no way that's the first time you've sang in front of people."

"I swear."

"You're a phenom," a guy next to her says. He has a sexily pinched face like Kurt Cobain's. His blond hair is messily styled, and he wears an oversized striped woolen sweater.

"This is Evan," Lacey says. "He's in the band I manage. Clarissa is the lead singer."

Clarissa puts down her mug to give a wave. "That was really amazing, Nico."

I'm still breathing heavily, the thrill of it all racing through my blood. I want to sing again and suck in another hit of the crowd's energy—my life forever changed now that I'd chase this new sober high.

"I left my body when I was up there," I say. "I can barely remember any of it."

"I'm sure you'll have many more out-of-body experiences," Evan says, tossing his bangs out of his eyes. They are the bluest I've ever seen, like an alien's. It hurts to look at them for too long.

"What's your band's name?" I ask, focusing on his chin instead.

"We've been through a few." He smiles like a child whose fingers have been caught in a cookie jar. "Rat Bastard, Gesundheit, Pablo Escobar's White Party, Sweet Baby Jesus and the Manger."

"Pablo Escobar's White Party was my favorite," Clarissa says.

"Ultimately, we went with Grenade Bouquets," Evan says.

"What kind of music?" I ask, trying to act normal while my heart still sounds like a machine gun firing off rounds.

"I'd say a blend of Smashing Pumpkins and Mazzy Star with a little Nirvana stirred in."

"Nico's on a road trip to Kurt Cobain's house," Lacey adds.

"Seriously?" Evan asks. "Rock on. Ever think about singing Nirvana songs?"

"All the time," I say.

"So…." Lacey says, looping her arm around mine. "Clarissa is headed to Europe for an art history trip for the next few weeks, but we have some gigs in Portland and Seattle lined up."

"Tough life, right?" Clarissa says, making a face.

"I was gonna do the singing duties," Evan says. "But I don't have a voice like yours."

I turn to Lacey. "Was this all, like, an audition?"

She winks. "I wanted to see if you had the chops."

I squeal just like Winter or Jeremy would have done.

"Yes, yes, yes." I can't contain my excitement,

knowing I should play it cool, but the adrenaline I'm experiencing doesn't have the ability to let me act chill.

"Hold on, hold on," Evan says. "We have to let you know what it entails."

"I don't care!"

"You might. For one, it doesn't pay anything."

"Don't care!"

"And two, we have a couple of our own songs but you'd sing the covers. I'll rattle off our setlists and you tell us which songs you know best."

"I'm an encyclopedia," I say. "If it's grunge, I know it."

"My bandmates Ed and Randy, the bassist and drummer, are at a bar now. Wanna meet them?"

I pinch myself, twisting the skin hard.

"What are you doing?" Evan asks, as I fall into his blue, blue gaze.

Could this all really be happening? I think, my organs dancing along to a sweet tune.

"Making sure I'm not dreaming," I say.

• • •

Everything is moving so fast. A few hours ago, I'd never even sung in front of an audience, now I'm in a band! Could I be any luckier? I warn myself to savor the moment and enjoy the fruits of my labor. We go to this bar Sips and find Ed and Randy splitting a pitcher of beer. Ed the bassist is a large dude taking up most of his side of the booth. Randy has a beard and a shaved head, seemingly older than the rest of them. It's clear that Evan runs the show with his pretty blues. Who wouldn't want to listen to him?

"We just heard Nico at the open mic at Café Hey and she rocked," Evan says, launching into a detailed explanation of my performance that he describes as electric and gloriously sullen.

"That's the kind of music we're making," Randy says. "Smashing Pumpkins, Mazzy Star, Nirvana hybrid."

"Yeah, Evan talked about it in that way."

"It's really just two gigs that Clarissa will miss. One in Portland and one in Seattle," Ed says and lets out a loud belch. "Sorry."

"There are ladies present," Lacey says.

"I don't see any."

"Sorry about Ed," she says to me. "He was raised in a barn."

Ed brays like a donkey. These guys are cool so far.

"We have two original songs that I wrote," Evan says.

"Oh wow, you're the songwriter too?" I gush. I tell myself to dial it back with ol' Blue Eyes before I make a fool of myself.

"Budding."

"Evan is brilliant," Clarissa says. "He's a poet."

The way she looks at him makes me wonder if the two are an item. I don't want a repeat of what happened in Ojai when I got attacked for stealing someone's dude and had trail mix thrown in my face. Besides I've sworn off dudes for the rest of this trip. Right?

"Cobain's the greatest poet of our generation," Evan says. "Like, he really digs into what it feels like to be us. How we're labeled slackers. A recession waiting for us when we graduate. What do people freakin' expect?"

"Totally."

"But he's also so honest. Like, he loves drugs."

"Who doesn't?" I say, and everyone laughs.

"I mean, drugs help him manage the pain he feels from being famous. He never chased fame. It found him. And that must be awful."

"I can't even imagine what it must be like."

The rest of the booth seems like they've vanished and it's just Evan and I alone musing about Cobain's insecurities.

"You know what Joplin, Hendrix, and Jim Morrison had in common?" Evan asks. I shake my head. "They were all twenty-seven when they died. Guess how old Cobain is now?"

I gulp, not wanting to hear anymore.

"Precisely." He takes a sip of beer. "Snuffed out at their peak. So that's what our music tries to embody. Chasing this flame that's bound to catch up with you."

"Grenade Bouquets are really good," Lacey says, popping up between us. "Like, I wouldn't manage them if they weren't. We've had about twenty gigs so far across the Pacific Northwest."

"I'm so bummed I have to go on this stupid art trip," Clarissa whines.

"Boo hoo, cry into your macaroni in Italy," Randy says.

"I'm gonna gain ten pounds," she says.

"The first gig is in Portland in two days so we gotta practice," Evan says. "You really up for it, Nico? We can go right now to Randy's garage just to make sure we gel."

I'd like to gel with you, I think, but I knock back

the rest of my beer, slam the glass down, and let out an earth-shattering belch to show that I can be one of the gang.

"Let's blow this popsicle stand."

• • •

We practiced all night in Randy's garage. Grenade Bouquets will be the opening band for both gigs so each setlist would be six songs in total, two of them Evan's original songs, "Everything's Chained" and "Stellar Swimmer," the first about an unpopular teenager who feels like he has no one to turn to, the second about a guy who tries to swim across the ocean only to drown (it's ironic). The covers we decide on are Nirvana's "Smells Like Teen Spirit," and "All Apologies," Smashing Pumpkins' "Disarm" and Mazzy Star's "Fade Into You." All of which I'd sung a thousand times before, into the mirror in my bedroom.

Standing in front of the microphone again, for the first time I worry that the performance at Café Hey might've been a fluke. But the instant Evan and Ed start thrashing their guitars, I belt out Nirvana like I've been performing my whole life. I'm surprised it comes so easily and that I don't feel shy singing in front of any of them. It's like when you drink a lot of water and once you pee for the first time you break the seal and are screwed for the rest of the day. I even add my own flourishes, giving "Smells Like Teen Spirit" more of a feminine energy that everyone seems to be into. Once again, I leave my body like I did before, shooting out of my skull once my lips hit the microphone only to return dazed and exhilarated when the song ends.

"I hate to say it, but I think she's better than Clarissa," Ed says, after Clarissa already left.

"We'll see," Evan says, but by the tone of his voice I can tell he agrees.

After playing through all the songs a bunch of times, the band is satisfied with how we sound and Randy suggests making Bloody Marys and watching the sunrise. We sit on his porch with spicy tomato clinging to the back of our throats as a glimmer of the sun fights its way through the clouds over Eugene's mountains. I think of watching the sunrise with Aunt Carly, which had been a little over a week ago but feels like a million years. I barely recognize that little girl who'd been afraid to go camping, now I'm a woman who has climbed mountains, sung her face off, and is momentarily joining a motherfucking band. I also haven't thought about Kristen since I left Café Hey, not needing her support at the moment, unsure if that's a good or bad thing.

"Dollar for your thoughts, Nico?" Evan asks, sitting beside me. He'd shaven and has a fresh and creamy smell.

"Just thinking how happy I am, and that I haven't been happy in a while."

"Lacey says you ran away from home."

"Oh."

"She didn't really go into it. I just asked what your deal is and she told me of your journey. Checking off bucket list items. Kind of awesome if you ask me."

"It has been."

I wonder if Lacey mentioned Kristen, but Evan

doesn't go into it so I doubt she did.

"Thanks for filling in," he says. "You'll really be saving us. Six songs in a row with me singing would be too much."

"You have a great voice too. I like the growl."

"Yeah, that's how Clarissa describes it."

I'm about to ask him if he and Clarissa are an item when Ed comes over with some Roman candles and the boys shoot them into the sky. I go over to Lacey and lean against her shoulder like she's Winter.

"Thank you. I can't tell you what this means to me."

"You're gonna be great."

"I think I just got nervous."

"Nonsense, you're a natural. And I'll be there for both shows so no worries."

I'm dying to ask the next question, but I pause like it just came to mind.

"Are Evan and Clarissa an item?"

"Used to be. She cheated on him."

"Ouch. Is he over her?"

"I think so, it was last semester. He's pretty isn't he?"

"He doesn't suck."

"So, Nico's into older men?"

"You guys are all just, like, a year and a half older than me."

She pulls my face in close and plants a kiss on my cheek.

"Go for him. If I wasn't solely into vag, I would've gone after him too."

"You're a...?"

"Yes. Strictly un-dickly. Tried men but they're not for me."

"My friend Winter and I have made out before."

"Ever kiss any other parts of her?"

"No."

"Ever think you want to?"

"Er...not really."

She slaps her knee. "Chill out, Nico. I'm not gonna roofie you in your sleep or anything. You're not my type anyway. I like 'em big, angry and butch. A girl that could throw me around."

"Ok cool."

"Just be yourself around Evan. Those are the kind of girls he likes."

I watch Evan shooting his Roman candle like he's an old-time gangster, the rainbow explosion reflected in his stellar eyes.

I ignore any nagging conscience telling me not to lose my focus. I lick my lips and get a tingle as I coolly whisper, "Evan, you're mine," while drawing a giant invisible heart around him.

A girl can only act serious for so long!

14

• • • • •

Fade Into You – Mazzy Star

The Grenade Bouquets set off for Portland in Ed's van. I'm cool following them in my car, but Evan suggests he rides with me to help with directions. I play it off like I'm fine without him, but inside I'm screaming yes, yes, motherfucking yes! Two unfiltered hours alone. And we could stop for a lunch break where I'll ask for a sip of his drink so my lips can touch where he left some spittle. I'm unsure what it is about him, but I'm already gaga.

"We can practice some of the songs," I say, once we start driving. "I have all of them on my mixtape."

I fast-forward until I reach Mazzy Star's luscious "Fade Into You." Hope Sandoval's pouty and breathy vocals fill the car as I sing along, mimicking her slinky sound. Evan sings along too, and I picture us touring the world together, bringing the lyrics he wrote to life as well. When the song ends, I turn down the volume.

"You've really made this car your home." Evan points at my Nirvana poster along with Aunt Carly's drawing and the various Polaroids from my travels as well as the picture of Kristen and me at Big Sur.

"Who's this cutie?" he asks, tapping my little nose in the picture.

"Me at nine. Big Sur trip."

"Awesome. It's amazing how little kids smile so big. Like, as adults we just can't stretch our mouths as much anymore. We've been through too much shit. Who's the friend next to you?"

"My sister," I gulp.

He looks closer. "Yeah, I can see the resemblance. Are you two close?"

"She died."

"Oh Nico, I'm so sorry."

"It happened a few months ago."

"A few months? How are you dealing?"

"I ran away from fucking home that's how I'm dealing!" I clench the steering wheel. "I'm sorry. Some days I'm good, some days I'm not."

He takes out two cigarettes from a pack in his front pocket. He lights them both and then puts one in my mouth.

"My brother was a soldier in the Army," he says, staring at the smoke curling from his cigarette. "During the Gulf War."

"That's rough, Evan," I say. This is not how I wanted our trip to go. More and more, I don't feel the need to talk about Kristen with everyone I meet. I'm tired of her taking over my life, creeping into my happiness. I eye the backseat in the rearview, expecting her to be there but it's vacant.

"He's still alive, but he's not the same person who

left. He lives at a VA hospital. My parents go see him, but it's too much for me. Like, he rants about conspiracies and he's on all these meds."

"When was the last time you saw him?"

"Not since I started school. I grew up in Boise, so that's where he is."

"Is that far?"

"It's far enough if you don't want to make the trip."

He takes another drag and then tosses the remaining half of the cigarette out of the window.

"The shitty thing is my dad was the one that pushed him to join the military. It's in our blood. Even after Chris came back all messed up, Dad still wants me to enlist. Like, for what purpose? Does he want two brain-damaged sons?"

He rubs his eyes and when he stops they're all red. "Screw our government. Kids like Chris gave their life for this country and what has it done for them?"

"It seems like things will be better with Clinton, right?"

"Those in power are all the same." He pats me on the leg. "I'm sorry for ranting. That's really terrible about your sister. If you ever need to talk about it...."

"I'd rather focus on good things right now. Like, tell me more about you."

I feel guilty for tossing Kristen aside, but she can't monopolize every experience on this trip. I have two hours alone with a great boy and want to maximize my time.

"Okay, well, I was very different early on in high school. Played soccer. Like, soccer was my life. But then, I got injured. Hamstring. I was out for the season;

this was my sophomore year. And I was really bummed so my mom got me a guitar. After I picked it up, I was like, screw soccer. First song I learned how to play was Bob Dylan's 'Mr. Tambourine Man'."

"I just learned guitar. Mother Love Bone's, 'Stargazer'."

"Yeah, I really get into Mother Love Bone. It's like having the cool card when you know them. Not everyone is aware of their brilliance."

Evan plays some air guitar. I can tell he's finally put thoughts of his brother away.

"But Boise is lame, like barely any music scene. It wasn't really until I got to University of Oregon that I met Ed and Lacey, people like me, and Clarissa too."

I wait to see if he'll say anything more about Clarissa. He stops playing air guitar and looks out of the window at the trees rushing by.

"We used to date. Clarissa was the first girl I thought I was in love with, but it wasn't love."

"I've never been in love," I say, and then immediately want to take it back.

"You're still young, Nico. Like, the shit you feel at sixteen, it's hormones, not love."

At first, I want to snap at him for talking to me like I'm a kid, but he's right. He seems so much older and wiser, someone I can learn from, someone who could change me.

With one eye on the road, I study the fine blond hairs on his chin, light like a duck's feathers.

"That's one of my bucket list items," I say, breathless.

"Falling in love?"

"Kissing someone I really like. That must sound

so stupid."

"Not at all. I've kissed so many girls I didn't even care about. It might have felt good, but there wasn't always a spark."

"Do you want to stop for some lunch?" I ask, seeing a road sign for fast food. The intensity of him being so close makes it hard to concentrate on the road. We pull into a McDonalds and he insists on paying for my Chicken McNuggets, fries, and a coke.

"BBQ sauce or Sweet and Sour?" he asks.

"Both."

"Ah, like to live on the edge?"

We take a seat by a window. A lull sits between us. I have a million things I think to talk about, but my brain can't concentrate. We dunk our nuggets, slurp our cokes, and finally he breaks the silence.

"I can't believe you've never sung in front of an audience before."

"I wasn't lying."

"No, I believe you. It's just, like, I need to play guitar in front of people. The rush I get from it. How could you keep that bottled up for so long?"

"I'm not sure." I slurp some more. He must think I'm a moron.

"What will you do after you sing at both our gigs?"

I shrug my shoulders.

"And once you go see Cobain's house, of course?"

"And when I finish all my bucket list items...?"

"Yup."

"I don't know. I haven't thought that far in advance. Everything is happening really quickly."

He points a forked nugget at me that drips with

BBQ sauce. "You're gonna keep singing, that's what. You live in L.A., Nico. There are a million bands you could join. Any would be lucky to have you."

"Maybe you should hire me permanently?"

He scratches at his neck. "Yeah, see, Clarissa is coming back and all."

"I'm just kidding. I'm not trying to take her spot."

"Like, we haven't even performed together yet–"

"I know, chill out. I need to finish school and all, like I couldn't just up and move to Eugene."

"Maybe you can come to UO for college? It's a pretty cool place. Big enough that you can find enough people like yourself. And plus, you already know us."

"My friends Winter and Jeremy back home don't wanna go to college. They think it's just frat parties and sororities and preppy kids."

"That's in movies. I've never been to one frat party."

"I have."

"Made out with a frat guy before?"

I nod.

"You little minx, Nico."

I want him to say something like, Here I thought I'd be your first college guy, or something along those lines, but he just goes back to eating his nuggets.

After a few more bites, he finally asks: "Is that your type? Chad the Frat President?"

"Do I look like that's my type? Give me a grungy and skinny boy like Cobain who doesn't always shower."

He sniffs his armpits. "I definitely didn't shower this morning."

"I haven't showered since California."

He chokes from laughing. "C'mon, let's get a move

on. The rest of Grenade Bouquets probably drove straight through and are waiting."

We leave and hit Portland about a half an hour later, the rain awaiting our arrival. The city looks perfectly gloomy, a much better match for me than shiny, glistening L.A.

Portland and Evan are already uplifting my mood. Singing in a few hours would be the delicious icing.

15

• • • • •

Smells Like Teen Spirit - Nirvana

Grenade Bouquets are playing at a venue called Freight Train, an eighteen and over place that makes you wear a wristband if you are twenty-one so you could drink. The bouncer doesn't blink at my Sasha Lioni ID, but the rest of the band has to show their real ones otherwise they won't be able to get paid. I share a beer at the bar with Randy who looks over thirty while the rest of them sets up. It's a small place, a tight stage with grungy pipes dripping moisture from the ceiling.

"How was your trip up?" Randy asks, running his fingers through his comb-over. "Evan's a sweetheart, isn't he?"

Randy looks at Evan with longing, which makes me wonder if I was guilty of staring at him like that too. It's also getting hard to keep track of who likes who in this band.

"He's pretty great."

We watch Evan tape the setlist to the stage.

"Did you guys hook up?" Randy asks, but I shake my head.

"It's just...." Randy leans in close. "Clarissa nearly destroyed him. Evan is better when he's not distracted."

"Or maybe you wanna be the one who's distracting him?"

I knock back my beer and get off the stool, imagining Randy having to pick his mouth up off the floor. I go over to where Lacey sits at a table with a calculator.

"I actually think we might not lose money with these two gigs," she says, and takes off her heavy glasses to massage her temples. "What the venues pay versus what we spend for gas usually puts us in the red."

"I have my dad's gas card," I say. "I can help pay our way to Seattle."

"That's sweet, but we'll be fine, Nico."

"So, Randy over there tried to cock block me."

"Yeah, he's gotta thing for Evan. I don't even know if he swings that way, Evan just seems to have that appeal for some people. Randy loves Evan. Clarissa still loves Evan. I love Clarissa."

"Really?"

"Yeah, I've already told her how I feel." Lacey mimes getting out a gun and pulling the trigger. "Shot down big time. But we're still cool so it's all right."

"I thought you liked girls big enough to throw you around."

"I do now. That's what I attract, so that's become my type."

My stomach growls and it feels like I have to go to the bathroom. I flap my nervous hands.

"You're gonna be great," Lacey says, rubbing my shoulder.

"You ever had a moment where you tell yourself, this is where my life begins?"

She looks me dead in the eye. "Nico, this is where your life begins."

"I gotta use the bathroom."

I rush inside the bathroom that's filled with graffiti. I sit on the toilet and have diarrhea city. Afterward, I splash some water on my face and square up in the mirror.

"You got this, Nico. You are one bad bitch."

I slap myself lightly across the face to get psyched up. As I leave the bathroom, I run into Evan.

"Hey," I say, shyly curling a strand of hair around my ear.

"Hey, you." He leans and kisses me on the cheek, his lips lingering for an extra second. "Kill it out there, you hear?"

"Aye aye, captain," I say, saluting.

I go back to the stage feeling like I'm flying. Evan comes back and we do a soundcheck. So far so good. People begin to show up. Teens but also older folks too. A sea of baggy jeans and flannels, wool caps due to the cool weather, girls in long floral dresses and black boots, pierced noses and lips, dyed hair like my own.

"I wanna thank everyone for coming," Evan shouts into his microphone. It's all really beginning. This isn't just some open mic night at a coffee shop. These people paid to be here and would boo our asses if we don't shine.

"We're Grenade Bouquets, and we like to start with a bang!"

I hear the crunchy guitar riffs of "Smells Like Teen Spirit" begin. Ed throttles the drums soon after. Now it's my turn. I close my eyes to transport myself away and give my voice more of a growly screech. As the song picks up, I thrash around the stage, wrapping myself around the mic stand and practically swallowing the microphone.

Open your eyes, I hear Kristen's voice say. Take it all in. A warmth spreads through my stomach knowing that she's here.

I moan as I do what she says and see the crowd of forty or so people banging their heads to our music and creating a beautiful mosh pit.

I yell over the wailing guitars and drumbeats. The crowd is screaming, begging for more.

"Yeah!"

"Wooooooo!!!!!!!" the crowd screams back.

I shout the end of the song and dive into the crowd. Strangers' hands lift me to the ceiling, cheering and carrying me along just as the lights go out and I'm dropped into darkness.

• • •

"Nico! Nico!" I hear Evan cry as feet trample over me. I don't know what's happening, but I can barely see anything until a lighter flashes and Evan's pretty face beams. "Are you okay?" he asks.

"I think."

I feel him lift me and I dangle in his lean arms. He

pushes past people rushing beside us as we charge for the exit door. The air hits my face as we leave, rain soaking me good. He catches his breath and I catch mine. Then he laughs.

"What a piece of shit venue, their lights went out."

"I think I went blind."

"Haha, you were so great out there."

"Really?"

"You blew the electricity."

"What?"

"Fucking rock star."

He kisses me hard, the rain coming between our make-out session. I clutch onto the back of his head and allow myself to be lost. While we kiss, there's no dead sister. My parents are still together, Winter and I never fought, and I'm not failing school. I'm the Nico I always should've been. When he pulls away, I become shattered. Sucked right back into reality's vacuum, a slave to my demons once again.

"Kiss me forever," I order him, thrusting back and falling gracefully into the ebb and flow of his guiding tongue.

Mentally I draw a line through the one bucket list item I've wanted the most to complete, save meeting Cobain of course.

• • •

Freight Train eventually gets their lights working again, and I'm assured that I had nothing to do with them going out. Some of the crowd left, since it takes about an hour to get everything running, but the majority comes back for more. They loved my Nirvana so Grenade Bouquets continues with "Come As You Are." This time when I sing, I don't need to close my eyes, confident with my abilities. I remember listening to the song in Ojai right before my road trip truly began, no idea what was about to occur. Right now, on this excursion, things couldn't be going better.

The mosh pit resumes, but I don't jump in, content to watch the crowd from high up, my voice getting them amped. I flow naturally with Evan's guitar, Randy's bass, and Ed's powerful drums. We are a unit. We are Grenade Bouquets, and I never want it to end, an eternity of singing my favorite songs.

We launch into "Disarm" by the Smashing Pumpkins next, a searing and painful song about disarming abuse with a smile, staying positive no matter what might be thrown at you. I channel Billy Corgan's nasal whine, thinking of my own parents that never abused but often neglected. When I'd return home, I decide to take the song's advice and disarm them with a smile rather than fight back with hatred.

Finally, we switch to Mazzy Star's "Fade Into You." I sit down on a stool for this one, thinking of the car ride earlier with Evan and then the kiss we just shared. I look over at him and we lock eyes, fading into one another, my new delicious soul mate. Maybe I could visit him from L.A. on the weekends. It's just another year and change before I'd graduate. Maybe I could even get an early degree and apply to U. of Oregon, although with my grade point average I know I wouldn't be accepted. I'd have to get my grades up over this semester and then try to apply early, and we could live in a dorm together and spend all day writing lyrics and having sex. I would have his children, I decide, and we'd name them Kurt and Courtney because we are cheesy like that.

I finish the song and I'm met with deafening applause, white-hot and shimmering. From heaven, Kristen must've been beaming after all my letdowns. Her and God finally deciding that I got my shit together and they wouldn't have to worry about me so much anymore.

I join the audience for the next two songs that Evan wrote, wanting to see him from the perspective of a fan. He owns the stage, his wavering voice fitting perfectly with the melancholic words. I snap a delectable photo as he's in mid-howl.

That's my man, I want to say to the crowd, who all stare at him with a god-like awe too. He chose to kiss ME and none of you other skanks, so back off!

When he finishes, he brings me back up on stage.

"Thank you, we're Grenade Bouquets." He waits for the cheers to die down. "I wanna thank Nico Sullivan, our guest lead singer for the night."

He bows down to me, and I hide my red face. Then he kisses me on the back of the hand like a courting prince would.

Afterward, the rest of the band congratulates me for doing so good. A few fangirls even want my autograph! I'd practiced my loopy signature many times, and they jump up and down after I sign.

"Could you get used to that?" Evan asks, and I nod. I bring him a beer as Sasha Lioni and we toast. "You're better than Clarissa."

Lacey overhears. "I agree, Nico, you're a natural."

"I'm not here to take anyone's spot," I say, catching Randy's eye. He seems to be the only one not going crazy over my performance.

Ed waddles over and lets out a belch. "I wanna leave first thing in the morning in case there's traffic. Early night kids."

We all give him a thumbs down, but then finish our drinks and go outside. All four of them usually sleep in the back of the van. Evan hangs back while Ed and Randy are setting up the beds.

"Or I can sleep with you tonight?" Evan says.

I imagine him impaling me with my feet slapping the ceiling. But I actually like this guy. I don't want either of us to just fuck and run. I don't want to be a maniac anymore.

"I mean, just sleep," he says, pushing his bangs out of his eyes. "Maybe some cuddling?"

"That's exactly what I was gonna say."

He holds my hand. "Okay, guys, we'll see you in the morning," he tells the rest of the band. Lacey winks at me while Randy doesn't even say goodbye. They pile inside the van and we make our way to my car.

I turn on the heat when we get inside, but Evan says we don't need it. We lie in the backseat covered by my flannels for blankets. He smells of beer and salty chips, his sweater musty and used. I ease my nose into the nape of his neck, and we both are so tired from the day that we fall asleep instantly.

I dream of sleeping with him in the backseat, the first time my dreams and reality actually link up.

16

• • • • •

All Apologies - Nirvana

I've never woken up in the arms of someone before, and it makes me never want to wake up solo again. Even though it's bitter cold outside, in my car, in our temporary home, I'm so wonderfully warm. Evan greets me with a morning kiss, our breaths rank but the kiss deep and meaningful. I reach over into my bag and squeeze some toothpaste on my finger, then give him some too. We semi-brush and then lose ourselves in the minty freshness of our licking tongues.

Evan gets us some breakfast sandwiches from a nearby Burger King and we munch them with sugary orange juice to wash it all down. Afterward, we leave Portland, and while I'm sad to see it go, I'm ready for Seattle.

"Will you come and see Cobain's house with me after the show?" I ask Evan. He's shaping his hair into a Mohawk.

"Like the new look?"

"It's too eighties," I say, reaching over and mussing

it up. His hair flops back over his eyes. "Much better."

"Sure, I'll see Cobain's house with you. But what if he's there and instantly falls in love with you when he opens the door?"

"Then you and I have had a good run."

He kisses me on the cheek over and over until I tell him to stop because it's distracting me.

"But don't really stop," I say, as he blows a raspberry on my neck that tickles. "Thanks for just sleeping with me last night and not trying to do anything more."

"I'm a gentleman."

"You are."

"So at the next rest stop we hit, I want to call my friend Winter. She and her mom have been covering for me with my parents. They think I'm staying at their house."

"El scandoloso!"

I pull over at a rest stop a few miles up and get out a bag of change to make the call. It's early enough in the morning that Winter possibly hasn't left for school yet, if she even decides to go today.

"Hello," she says.

"Wiiiiinnnnttttteeerrrrrr," I hum, so amped to hear the sound of her voice. "I miss you."

"Nico?"

"The one and only."

"Nico, listen–"

"So I met this boy," I say, speaking faster than ever. "His name is Evan and plays in this band called Grenade Bouquets–"

"Nico, I have to tell you–"

"Just wait. He is awesome! We slept together last

night in my car, but like, didn't screw. Actually slept! It was so romantic. And what's even cooler, I sang FOUR songs last night at a venue with his band. Like, I ruled the stage. It was...it was unreal. There was a mosh pit! And the lights blew out!"

"Your parents know you ran away," she says, sighing.

"What?"

"Evidently, the school called their house since you were out for over a week. I guess all the times I'd skipped, it was never that many days in a row. Anyway, your folks came over huffing and puffing and tore Edina a new asshole. Like, they were livid. Your mother had this scary vein throbbing on her head."

My stomach drops. "Oh, shit."

"Yeah, I told them you were fine and checking in with me. But they didn't care. You have to call them ASAP."

"I can't call them now."

"Nico, they'll be up my ass if you don't."

"I'm playing this gig in Seattle today and then Evan and I are going to see Kurt Cobain's house."

"They've called the police."

"Did you tell them where I am?"

"I said you were in Northern California the last time we spoke. They'll know you were arrested in San Francisco."

"So I'm a million miles from there now."

"I told them you were headed to Seattle for the grunge scene there."

"Damn you, Winter!"

"The cops were here. It was a mess. And I had all this pot in my room. I got nervous."

"I'll just have to be careful in Seattle around cops if they're looking for me."

"I think it's time for this fantasy to end and for you to come home."

"What's that, bitch? Let's not forget that this was your brilliant idea."

"I know! And it sounds like you've done a ton of bucket list items already. You proved your point. Your parents give a shit and they've gone hella ballistic."

"This isn't about them at all!"

"Nico, you always say that they don't pay enough attention to you. Especially after Kristen–"

I want to slam down the phone. "Don't bring up Kristen! Like, I'm having an awesome time, and I'm finally not sad right now. Can I just have that for, like, a few days? Is that too much to ask?"

"The police are gonna keep coming over and grilling me and Edina. She's had terrible migraines since."

"I will call the 'rents tomorrow. Just let me have one more day."

"Fine, Nico, but you better do it."

The phone clicks, and I don't want to put in more quarters. "Winter, I gotta go. I'm sorry that this all got so crazy."

"It's okay," she says. "I'm glad you're having an adventure. But if you don't call them tomorrow, I'll never speak to you again."

"Somehow I don't believe that."

"Okay, fine, but I'll be really pissed and I'll make you my slave to do whatever I want till I feel like the apology is sufficient."

"You rock, Winter."

"Love you, girl. Have a great show tonight. So cool you sang by the way. I know that's been your dream for a long time."

"I left my body. And the crowd was so into it. I even signed autographs."

"I can always say I knew you when."

"Bye, love."

"Smooches, you delinquent."

I hang up, a little shaken by what I'd just learned. For one second, I feel guilty about my parents freaking out; but they deserve it. When I call them tomorrow, I'll deal with their bullshit. At least I'd have one last day of this wild ride.

As I walk back to my car, I could hear Evan playing Nirvana's "All Apologies." I flop back into the car.

"So I just talked to my friend Winter. The school contacted my parents and they fully know that I ran away. So now I'm an official runaway, I guess. Score!"

I laugh, but when I look over at Evan, his face has turned white like he has a terrible stomach flu. His eyes are raw and red.

"What the hell is wrong?" I ask, as a chill crawls up my skin.

Cobain's voice is still trapped in the car singing about the sun and being married and buried.

"What?" I say, raising my voice.

"He shot himself," Evan says, erupting into tears.

"Who's dead?"

But then my body goes cold. I can't feel my heart beating. My hands turn numb. My breath vanishes. Ice in my veins. Blood frozen. Head throbbing. The world appears as if I'm looking through the wrong side of pair of binoculars.

Had I died too?

All and all is all we are.

Cobain's ghost sings the final lyrics before the song ends and a dead silence swallows us both up.

SIDE B

• • • • •

April 1994

17

• • • • •

Deathwish - L7

Neither of us knows what to say as Evan and I continue on to Seattle. He has to drive because I'm crying so hard I don't trust myself behind the wheel. I keep hoping I'll wake up, and Cobain's death is a bad nightmare. I know that he'd been in a drug and alcohol coma about a month back, but he'd gotten out of rehab so I assumed everything was okay. There have been rumors that Nirvana was breaking up because they've canceled their current tour, but over the years there's been so much gossip about the band ending, it's hard to trust what's real.

We listen to the news report on the radio. A VECA Electric employee who'd arrived at the house that morning to install security lighting saw Cobain not moving inside. He found a suicide note with a pen stuck through it lying in a flower-pot. A shotgun was resting on Cobain's chest, and he had a visible wound on his head. The King County Medical Examiner noted puncture wounds on the inside of both his right and left elbow, likely from heroin.

Evan switches from the news to stations that only play Nirvana. In every lyric, I hear Cobain's pain, a foreshadowing of this day. "Lithium," "I Hate Myself and I Want to Die," "Serve the Servants," "Stay Away." The signs have all been there. Why did they release him from rehab? They should've held him for longer if he was a danger to himself. His daughter Frances is just a baby. How could he leave her and all of us as well?

I need to be inebriated, something to take the edge off. I reach into my duffel bag and pull out a joint and don't even bother rolling down the window. As I inhale, I long for my lungs to burst—an easy path to death. First River Phoenix, then Kristen, now my sweet Kurt; everyone I love taken from me. I have a paranoid fear I'll soon be next. My seventeenth birthday is three months away, the Grim Reaper is waiting with his evil scythe.

I look over at Evan who's been able to maintain his sadness. He appears more shell-shocked than distraught. I want him to smother me, to take away my pain with his kiss, his caress, his body crushing mine into oblivion.

"Pull over," I say, with my hand on his knee.

"What?"

The radio blasts "Frances Farmer Will Have Her Revenge On Seattle."

"I need you."

I run my hands up and down his leg, and he squirms in place.

"Nico, stop."

I rub harder, feeling him getting aroused through his jeans.

"I'm driving."

"So what? So what? So what?" I'm screaming, a violent banshee. If he doesn't screw me right there and show me what love can truly be, I decide I'll kill him by grabbing the wheel and flipping the car. "I need you inside of me."

He swats me away, a stinging rejection. I take it as a challenge and cling to his side, my tongue in his ear.

"Nico!"

The car wavers from lane to lane. He pushes me off. He's yelling at me, but I block my ears. I retreat to the window and let my head rest against the cool moisture. I wonder what would happen if I bash my face through it.

"Fine," I say. "Never speak to me again."

He grips the steering wheel, his knuckles blinding white. "I don't want you like this."

"I don't want you at all!" I snap, chomping at my teeth and pretending it's his heart. I pick back up the joint that's resting on the dash and suck and suck until I reach a state of numb.

In my semi-conscious stupor, I vacillate between rage for Cobain taking the easy way out by killing himself and an extreme sorrow for someone who seemingly had everything but was truly miserable. We are responsible for his passing. We built him up into the god he never wanted to be. We leeched on and sucked out every last drop of blood until there was nothing left. Why couldn't he have escaped to some remote country and written poetry for the rest of his life? There'd been so many moments when I considered giving up, exhausted from missing Kristen, and I played his songs to be seduced by someone as miserable. But he'd been worse off, never made for this world, my beautiful, rotting blond saint. What if I'd been able to meet him and rock away his blues?

I'm pissed for not running away sooner. I should've found him because he needed me. Now it's too late.

I float out of my spoiled dreamland to the crunching sounds of "Smells Like Teen Spirit." Just yesterday, I'd sung the shit out of that song, happier than I'd ever been, my brilliant high now torn down.

"We'll give him a true tribute tonight," Evan says. I can tell he's nervous to speak to me, unsure how I'd react. The thought of singing later makes me want to rip out my vocal cords. The thought of doing anything too draining to even ponder. I could basically sleep, and I could get bombed. I could screw, and nothing else.

"Nico?" Evan asks, his voice trembling. "We'll channel his spirit tonight, right?"

"How can you even think about your stupid band?" I ready a hunk of my spit to launch in his face.

"Our fans will want it."

I let out a huff. "Fans? Cobain had legions, you have a couple of groupies. You're a poor comparison."

His face muscles clench. "I'm not trying to compare."

"I was drawn to you because you look like him, but strip all that away and you're ordinary."

"Why are you being so mean?"

"Because nothing matters anymore. Cobain's dead, my sister too. Your brother is the mayor of Crazy Town."

"Don't talk about Chris." His blue eyes cut me, knives in my chest. I love my viciousness, longing to obliterate.

"He would've been better off dying in combat."

"Shut the hell up."

"I hope your dick falls off."

He cranks up "Smells Like Teen Spirit" to drown out my terrible ass. I still shoot him with cruel jabs, but my voice becomes muffled until finally I give up, grab a sweatshirt from my duffel and hide inside of it, retreating into my own little isolated world, a much better place than where I'm dwelling.

• • •

We drive to 171 Lake Ishington Blvd East. Cobain's home is surrounded by cars and reporters and kids like me bawling. I need to run to them and share in their anger. Evan isn't acting upset enough, a foolish traitor. He goes to take my hand as we step outside, but I decline. We won't enter the tragedy as a couple because we aren't one. We've been a façade.

The reporters all have perfect hair and wear suits and blouses. They couldn't be more removed from Cobain. I hear one of them say: "Most people over thirty probably didn't know who Kurt Cobain really is, but he had a hold over the disaffected youth that encompasses Generation X." What a stupid thing to say. I picture tearing off the reporter's head and tossing it in the bushes, watching his body spin around like a decapitated chicken.

People leave flowers by the door like that means anything. It makes me angry at myself for bringing peonies every time to the Viper Room as if River Phoenix was looking down and appreciating my empty gifts. Cobain was shy and wanted his privacy; he would've hated this kind of outpouring. Conversations I overhear all seem to focus on who's the biggest fan and how much Nirvana saved them. One girl wears a Nirvana T-shirt and has the names of their songs sewn all over her backpack. She's telling another girl whose bottom lip is full of piercings that she had tried to kill herself, but Nirvana's music made her want to live. Now she isn't sure. They hug and cry and curse the sky. Evan puts his arm around me.

"Do you want to stay or should we go?" he asks. I have no desire to even be around him, his arm like a snake coiling my neck. "What? What did I say now?"

I'm shivering. "I'm, like, dead inside right now."

"What do you want me to do?" he asks, trying to eke out an attempt at a smile. "I'm just trying..."

"I asked you before in the car to screw me and you wouldn't so what's the point of you?"

"You're upset."

"I'm a beast right now, a terrorist, and you're in my line of fire."

"I can take it, Nico."

"No you can't, you're too weak."

I'm really saying that to myself but I don't care. I wrench away from Evan and push through the crowd until I can get a glimpse of Cobain's house, an ordinary suburban place like my own that encapsulated the greatest person of the late twentieth century.

Bits of puke curl up my throat and I swallow

them back down, letting the bile fester and simmer. "Cover me in puke," I say, out loud. Next to me are two older guys in their twenties, coated in dirt that looks like faded shoe polish. One has forest green dreadlocks, the other a safety pin through his nose. Their eyes flicker between inebriated and aware. Safety Pin holds up his palm and I place mine against it. He smells like a sidewalk street, spittle caught in his unruly beard.

"Wanna get destroyed with us?" he asks, blinking his creamy eyes.

"Only if you promise me absolute destruction," I reply.

"Hey, wait, I gotta new complaint," he sings, his voice riddled with smoke. His hand cups the back of my head and his mouth widens. He brings me in for a kiss and I long to be swallowed, imagining perfect little Kristen covering her eyes in heaven and then having Cobain pry her fingers apart to witness my downward spiral.

Safety Pin devours me with a kiss, his tongue full of bumps like he's eaten sand. I puke up again a little, passing my sickness to him. He tastes like he's on his last days. I'm so jealous of his rotting corpse, ready to crumble to dust right there.

I feel myself being pulled away, but I lunge for more of his disgusting breath. When I spin around, Evan stares back at me like he doesn't recognize me at all.

"You don't know me," I say.

"Nico, what is wrong with you?"

I try to claw away from him, but he's too strong despite his thin frame.

"If you won't torture me, I'll find someone who will," I screech.

"Stop it, stop it." He's trying to shake the sickness out of me, but I've already been infected. I'm poison and everyone I adore is bound to end up ruined as well.

"Run away from me if you know what's good for you," I rave, an out of control animal now, my sanity left on the highway, on the street in Laurel Canyon where Kristen jogged her last run. Where is she now when I need her so?

"No, I'm not leaving you like this," Evan yells into my ear. I knee him in the balls and take off away from the crowd, collapsing to the ground and skinning my knee badly. A streak of red paints the dirt.

A trio of two guys and a girl watch my ungraceful fall. The three of them are hugging as if they're holding onto each other for dear life. I plead to them with my eyes to join, and miraculously they let me in their circle. We breathe life back into one another. They rub my back, my neck, clearly on something that I want to be a part of.

"Give me whatever you have," I whisper into one of the guy's ears. He procures a pill that I pop in my mouth before I even have a chance to see what it is. I crunch down, its venomous paste stuck in my teeth. With each lick, a shiver tingles down my spine. I fall into the drug, become lifted off my feet. When they tell me to come with them, I nod.

"Where are we going?" I ask.

"To a room where we can sink," the girl says. Her head is shaved and she has one long braid that trickles down to her chest. She isn't wearing a bra and one of her boobs has popped out. I tweak her nipple and she smiles through tears. A van pulls up, the doors opening as the two guys lead me inside.

Through the back windows, I swear I can see Evan running, his palm outstretched for me not to go. But then he vanishes and so do I.

Cobain had let out a rallying cry to join in his self-destructive blitz and I will comply.

18

• • • • •

Fast and Frightening – L7

I peer out of the window in the back of the van. The pill I've swallowed starts to kick in, shapes and colors swirling. A cop car blips down the street, and I remember that my parents probably had the Seattle police looking for me. "Speed up!" I yell to whoever is driving. "The police!" The girl with long braid cackles, one of the guys licking at her throat. The other watches in fascination. I jump in his lap, hoping he can protect me from the law. I'm not ready to go home. I flirt with the thought of never returning, letting this van take me to a new life where I don't have to bother with sobriety.

The guy wears a ratty T-shirt that asks: Is This The Future? I reply that it is, ready for whatever outcome.

"Are you my future?" I ask, running my fingers through his beard and feeling like I'm releasing tiny bugs from being trapped.

"No, because the world is ending," he says, crying. So we cry together until our tears mix and become indistinguishable.

"I love you," he says, moving in for a kiss. We stay in place for the rest of the ride: our mouths united, breathing in each other's melancholy.

The van pulls up to a building that seems like it's being renovated. We climb an endless staircase and reach an apartment that's full of long hallways. I have to step over bodies that are passed out on the floor. One grabs onto my foot and tries to take a bite as if it's a zombie. I kick it in the face and continue on, following the two guys and the girl with one braid.

A large room with sunlight beaming in houses a few other souls draped across the soiled furniture. A guy and a girl are half-naked, giving each other a massage, their eyes rolling. The air stinks of cigarettes and neglect, the floor sticky with syrup. Slapping noises beat against the walls, sounding like the place is haunted. This is exactly where I want to be.

The braided girl leads me over to the window. She tells me I have pretty hair. One of the guys comes up behind me and rests his chin on my neck. He has another pill. It drops in my palm.

"What is it?"

"Pain management," another guy says. He had emerged between my legs like a merman rising from the sea.

"It's calling to you," the braided girl says.

"I miss her," I reply, because the emptiness I feel is so heavy I have to acknowledge its presence. I could try to put it aside, but it will always be there for the rest of my life, however short that might be. And now even Kristen's ghost has decided to disappear too, just when I'm the most desperate for its presence, my powers of conjuring muted.

"No, sweetie, he died," the girl says, caressing my cheek. Her fingernails are blackened like she's been crawling through ink. "Cobain."

She places a pill on one guy's tongue who shakes and laughs like he's being tickled by the devil. His marble eyes roll to the back of his skull and he lies down as if he's floating on a cloud. Then she repeats the ritual and gives another pill to the second guy. They curl up next to each other like two little kids snuggling in bed. One of them even pops his thumb in his mouth.

"Are you ready?" she asks.

Whatever remains of me is so far gone. I try to call for Kristen, screaming about saying no to drugs that every cheesy sitcom episode warned about; but Nico won't listen. She wants to decay. Someone tells me the first pill they gave me was just a tease, this one the real enchilada.

The braided girl opens my mouth for me with her fingers.

"It's bliss," she says, her words drawn out and spacey.

The L7 song "Fast and Frightening" pumps in my head about a girl they called "an evil machine." That's me now. One swallow and there'd be no going back.

The door to the room swings open and a man in blue rushes inside. He's ranting. I can barely see straight, but he appears to be an officer. They have found me.

"Nooooooooo," I scream, knocking the pill out of Braided Girl's hand. I grab her wrist. "Don't let them take me."

"You're whacked."

I slap her across the face, sending her to the floor.

The man in blue is coming for me. He lunges, but I dive down and scurry away on my stomach. I dash into a side room where a loud fan blows dirty air and an emaciated girl draws all over herself with a pen.

"I'm hiding from the police," I tell her.

"Lock the door," she replies, barely summoning enough energy to speak.

I do what she says and run to the window. There's no sign of a cop car. I take a deep breath, relieved.

A loud knocking pounds from outside.

"Oh shit, they've found me." I'm shaking her by the shoulders; her head flopping around like a broken doll's. "I'm not ready to go back home. I wanted to be better when I returned. That's the point of all of this. But it's worse than ever. She's gone. I can't even imagine her anymore. I'm losing the sound of her voice!"

"You're mad."

The pounding gets louder.

"Nico!" I hear a muffled voice say. The police officer knows who I am, this journey about to end.

"Nico!"

A body bashes into the door, the lock starting to give. I hide behind the girl who's barely over a hundred pounds. The door flings open to reveal Evan.

"I'm getting you out of here," he says.

"No, this is my home now!" I scream, using the thin girl to buffer us. The girl starts freaking out and manages to squirrel herself away.

I feel myself being picked up and carried out of the room. I kick and yell as Evan brings me into a bathroom. Mold has destroyed the walls and the shower drips, drips, drips. He throws me in the bathtub and turns the faucet as tan water pours over my face.

"What did you take?" he asks me.

"Fuck you!"

"Nico, what did you take?"

"A tiny pill that loves me more than you ever could."

He crams his fingers down my throat until I puke up what looks like white snot all over him.

"Fuck, Nico, Jesus."

I hack and cough and wipe away my awful sickness. He finds a grimy towel and cools down my forehead, then strips off my shirt that had caught the brunt of my puke too.

"Why does everything have to die?" I ask.

"I don't know."

I find his blue eyes and let them return me to reality.

"I'm dying too."

"You're not, Nico."

"Kristen…she died of a brain aneurysm, my grandfather also. There won't be any escape."

He crawls into the tub with me and turns off the water.

"That doesn't mean you're dying."

"But everyone around me is leaving. What if I want to go as well?"

"You don't. You have so much life left, and yeah it sucks that your sister won't have that, but it doesn't mean you don't deserve to."

"I'm a terrible person."

"You've been dealt with too much to handle. Like Cobain."

I've forgotten about Kurt's suicide and howl at being reminded of it again.

"But he's happier now," I say. "I'm sure of it."

"He's dead, Nico."

"But when life is pain…"

"Your life isn't pain."

I push him away. "Don't tell me what I'm going through. Everyone wants me to shut up and get over things. You, Winter, Jeremy, my parents. I've become a burden."

"There's no rulebook that tells us how to deal with tragedy. But time…"

"Don't say it heals everything."

"It will. When my brother first came back different, I was devastated. And I still am, but I don't think about him every second anymore."

He reaches into his pocket and takes out his car keys.

"I followed that van in your car. Let me get you out of here. Don't worry about singing at the show. I'll get you a hotel room and you can just sleep. Then maybe we should call your parents to let them know what's going on. They're probably very worried."

"I am not calling my parents."

"Nico, if the police are looking for you they must be worried sick."

"Good, let them."

"Imagining the worst–"

"The worst has happened, Cobain's dead!"

"You didn't know him. Sure, you idolized him like I did. But he isn't a real person in our lives. And he took the easy way out."

"Give me my keys."

"You're in no condition to drive."

"Give me my keys, you goddamn thief."

I charge for the keys and he yanks them away. He's spooked because I've let the beast out again, ready to take no prisoners. He might've made me vomit, but lingering pieces of the pill still permeate through my system. And there's no fucking way I'm ready to give up on running away. I'll keep heading north until I eventually fall into the ocean.

He tries to contain me with one arm, but I'm too strong. I gnash my teeth and push him into the tiled wall. He hits his head, the keys spilling from his hands. I scoop them up and leap out of the bathtub. I catch him looking at me, begging me not to go, but my legs won't listen. They carry me out of the bathroom, through the endless hallways and zombies laying booby-traps, to the front door that leads to a descending staircase and finally the success of reaching outside, the wind slapping against my face, my teal blue car winking in the sun. I get behind the wheel and tear out of there just as Evan appears in the rearview like the T-1000 from Terminator 2 out to get me. I floor it as he tries to chase me, but I'm too fast, making a hard left and putting him out of my sight for good.

19

• • • • •

Doll Parts - Hole

On vacations, Kristen and I were forced to spend time together once our gap in ages made us less close. These happened infrequently since Dad rarely took off from work. But once a year, we planned a trip. Santa Barbara. Lake Tahoe. A jaunt to London. Our final one last summer had been to Puerto Vallarta, Mexico. We slipped into our usual roles: Mom the nag, Dad the mope, Kristen the star, me a surly blob. Resorts were the best because everyone could do their own thing. Mom and Dad often fought so neither of us wanted any part of that. We were allowed to split up, but not in town for fear that we could be kidnapped by banditos (literally the words that came out of my mother's mouth).

There weren't that many places to hide from each other at the resort so we drank virgin pina coladas by the pool and worked on our tans. In no time, Kristen turned golden and shiny where I became red and bloated from my period.

"Why do the 'rents even try anymore?" I asked, as we lounged on plastic chairs.

She pulled off her sunglasses and shielded her eyes from the sun.

"I think Dad feels like he's a good parent by showing us the world."

"He sucks donkey balls as a parent. I bet he doesn't even know the color of my eyes."

"Sure he does," Kristen said. "They're black like your heart."

This had been a semi-joke we often shared. How one day I woke up an evil version of my old self. I hated everything, hid in my room, listened to angry music, and cursed like a sea wench.

I spied the Walkman on her chest. "What are you listening to?"

"You're just gonna make fun."

"I promise I won't." I took out the cassette tape to find The Sign by Ace of Base. "You own their whole tape?"

She swiped it back. "It's shiny, it's pop. We're in Mexico. I don't want to listen to a singer who wants to slit their wrists."

"But you're so much smarter than Ace of Motherfucking Base."

"Nico, people can like different things. Your job isn't to police the world on how cool everyone should be."

"Fine," I said, throwing up my hands. "We won't talk music. Any boys in your life?"

"I have college applications coming up, so I don't have time for a relationship."

"Who said anything about a relationship?"

Kristen was mega gorgeous. Blond hair out of a shampoo commercial. Legs that never seemed to end. It was as if she'd taken all the good genes and there wasn't much left over for me.

"You are so hot, Kristen. How about just getting good and dicked?"

Her face scrunched up. "The way you talk sometimes, Nico."

"Oh, get that lifetime achievement award out of your ass."

I grabbed our drinks and made my way to the bar. Using my Sasha Lioni alias, I had the bartender fill it with mucho tequila. It'd still be sweet enough that I doubted Kristen would notice. When I brought it back, she sucked it down like a thirsty bitch.

"Did it get hotter out here?" she asked between hiccups.

"Yeah, we're in fucking Mexico in the summer, what do you expect? Lemme get you another."

Three tequila coladas later, we were both shitfaced and hugging.

"I hate you but I love you," I said.

"What?" she belched and smelled her hair. "Is there taco meat in my hair?"

"No, but listen. I was serious when I said you need to get with some boys. You're gonna look back at high school and all you'll have to show for it are great grades."

"And being captain of track and field and volleyball, and I starred in the production of Threepenny Opera, and I head up the social actions committee and..."

"All right this isn't an interview, but what about fun? Do you have fun?"

She gazed at me with her hands on my shoulders. "I'm going to be a doctor."

"So?"

"So it's, like, a really important profession. I don't have time to have fun. Do you have fun? What do you do with those two sewer rats you're friends with?"

"For fun?" A montage of Winter, Jeremy and I getting super blasted ran through my mind. The question was never: what do we want to do? It was always: what should we ingest to enhance this experience? "I get drunk, I get high."

"See, I don't need substances. Life is stimulating enough."

I mimed the act of puking.

"Well, you're drunk right now, bitch," I said, pointing in her face.

"What?"

"Those last three drinks were full of tequila and you didn't even know. Guess you weren't able to diagnose that, Dr. Loser."

"I'm gonna be sick."

She leaned over the chair and vomited in the pool. Little children screamed and mothers gave us scorned looks. Kristen covered her face.

"Thanks, Nico, I feel awful."

"All right, take it down a notch. It's not like I boiled your bunny."

Mom and Dad arrived at the pool with wonderful timing just as Kristen lay down moaning.

"What's wrong, Kristen?" Mom asked, feeling

her forehead.

"Nico got me drunk."

"Nico!" Mom snapped, looking like she wanted to spit on me. "Are you drunk too?"

"No," I hiccupped.

"Up," Dad said, yanking my arm.

We were brought back to our room. Kristen spent the rest of the day puking and my punishment was to stay and listen. After she had nothing left in her, she crawled into bed and hid under the covers.

I placed my hand on her back. "I'm sorry, Kristen."

"You're reckless. You ruin everything."

"I know," I said, gnawing on a fingernail.

"Just stay away from me for the rest of the trip. I'd rather hang out with Mom and Dad."

"Ouch."

She kicked at me until I was forced off the bed. I shut out the lights and left her alone, meandering back to the bar where I continued my research of tequila coladas and their effects on my already twisted brain.

• • •

I'm thinking about our Mexican trip as I drive through the streets of downtown Seattle blasting Hole's "Doll Parts," the car swerving from lane to lane. People rubberneck as I speed by, and I yell that someday they'll "ache like I ache." A morose haze has sunken over the city, Cobain's death seen on weeping faces. I don't want to hit any of them with my car, but I long for a crash, my body incinerating.

"Don't do it," a voice says.

Kristen sits in shotgun putting on her seatbelt. She inspects her hair in the rearview, making sure it's perfectly straight, even her ghost a control freak. Somehow, I knew it'd be back.

"You're already dead," I say. "What does it matter if we crash?"

"Stop the car and give me the keys."

I hack like a cat coughing up a hairball in response.

"Don't you want me to join you?" I joke.

"No, Nico, I..."

I slam on the horn. "Kristen, I was doing okay, like, I'd reached a place where I was dealing with you being gone and then Cobain had to go and fucking die too!"

"He's just a rockstar."

"He is everything, especially after you left. His lyrics are exactly what I'm feeling. Like, he was speaking to me when no one would listen."

"Good, I'm glad you had that. But now he's gone and you have to move on."

"I don't know if I can."

I press down on the accelerator, the car roaring, swerving between other frightened drivers.

"Then you're a coward."

"Screw you!"

"If you died, Nic, I would've been devastated, but I'd make sure to spend the rest of my days truly living."

"Why do you think I have a freaking bucket list?"

"Is dying included on it?"

"It's a recent addition."

Courtney Love wails, I fake it so real I am beyond fake. Someday you will ache like I ache.

"What is the point of your bucket list?" she asks,

raising her voice. Kristen rarely yelled. It always took a lot to shake her up.

"Because I'm headed for an early grave too."

She pinches my arm. "No, you are not. You're not me. You won't die at seventeen."

"Who says?"

She points to the sky. "The big guy."

"Bullshit."

"You're gonna be a mother, a grandmother, you're gonna be a famous singer. I see you singing and you have it, that spark. You'll put out albums, and you'll be fulfilled without me there."

"But I feel guilty."

She strokes my hair. "For what? Nothing is your fault."

"I'm sorry I got you drunk that time in Puerto Vallarta."

"Vomit under the bridge," Kristen says, smiling. "And I knew about the mixtape."

I turn away from the road, my jaw hanging open. "Wait, what?"

"I knew you were making it for my birthday. I saw it on your bed when I was passing by your room. I would've been really excited about it. I would've listened to every song. And I bet I might've even liked one or two. But I'd never let you know that."

I sniff up tears. "Oh, Kristen."

"It was very sweet. And you were a good sister. We were just really different as we got older. Can't blame either of us for that. But now you have to promise me something."

"Anything."

"Nico, watch out!"

"Huh?"

"Watch out," she yells, throwing her hands over her face.

I look back at the road just as the car shoots off the main street running headfirst into a lamppost. My head snaps against the steering wheel.

My face rests against the car horn playing its mournful song. Onlookers collect around to witness my destruction. Out of puffy slits, I see them descend toward me until darkness eclipses them all.

20

• • • • •

Disarm – Smashing Pumpkins

Flitting in and out of consciousness, I remember being pulled from the car, unsure how bad it's been totaled. Evan is there, telling me to stay calm. Hole's "Doll Parts" still blasts and a crowd has formed. I wonder if scattered parts of me are all that remain. I don't know if an ambulance is taking me to the hospital.

I wake with a throbbing head, the room dark, the bed uncomfortable. I want to know what happened, but I'm so tired so I close my eyes and go back to sleep.

In the morning, a nurse rustles me awake. She looks like a cherub: rosy cheeks, wide eyes, little baby arms. I want her to swaddle me. She says my friend had brought me in and that I'd been drugged and fell down, hitting my head. No mention of a car. The doctors stitched up the wound. There is no sign of a concussion. She asks if there's anyone I want to call and explains that my friend has been here all-night waiting for me to wake-up.

"No one to call," I say, my throat so dry. "Can you send him in?"

Evan appears a few minutes later, shyly peering at the door with an unsure wave. I immediately start welling up.

"What really happened to me?"

He creeps inside as if he's been waiting for my approval. He rubs his hands together nervously.

"I found you in your car. You had hit your head against the steering wheel. The keys were in the ignition, but you hadn't driven anywhere."

"Shit." I readjust myself, my body sore. I put my hand up to my forehead and realize there's a bandage. Somehow the vision of Kristen saved me. She'd prevented me from taking off and destroying myself and possibly anyone else in my path. I wonder how many more times she'd return when I'm in need, or if she'll eventually give up on my wayward ass.

"I followed you into that squatter's place. What the hell, Nico? People lying around looking brain dead. You can't just be getting into random people's vans."

"Is Kurt Cobain still dead, or was that a hallucination?"

He shakes his head ominously.

"Fuuuuuucccccckkkkkk."

I slide under the covers, deciding I'd remain there forever to avoid the cruel world. Evan peels them back and disarms me with his smile.

"Inch over," he says, lying next to me.

"I was so shitty to you. Like, all those terrible things I said."

"I'm a big boy and can take it."

"Your show!" I say, jolting up.

"It was canceled cause of what happened with Cobain. There was a memorial for him instead. The rest of Grenade Bouquets went."

"I think you guys are a hella dope band, and you're gonna be huge. I never meant to make you feel small."

"Our best show was still the one you sang at."

My face reddens. "Such a charmer."

"That's my job." He kisses me on the cheek. "Listen, Nico..."

"Uh-oh, that's how my Dad starts a sentence when there's serious shit to discuss."

"I don't want to tell you how to live your life, but maybe it's time to end your bucket list adventure and go home. What other items do you really want to check off?"

I mentally go through my list and can't think of anything else. Reaching Cobain's house had been the final event.

"I'm scared to return to L.A.," I admit.

"Why?"

"Because there's nothing really for me there. What if I stay in Eugene with you? I could get a GED."

"You mean Good Enough Diploma?"

"Yeah, it would be good enough. What else am I really gonna learn at school that I need? Algebra? History? BFD—Big Fuckin Deal."

"Clarissa is coming back, remember?"

"And you want to get with her again, right?"

"No, it's not like that. But she's our singer. We started Grenade Bouquets together. It's her dream as well."

"But I'm better than her."

"You're definitely talented. There's a rawness about your singing that's powerful, but you need to practice a ton more too. I don't want to be responsible for you dropping out of school."

"Look, no one tells me what to do. I'd be doing it because I want to."

He doesn't answer and I know I'm losing him. He's not ready to take on a runaway train of a sixteen-year-old, and I can't blame him, since I could barely handle myself.

"Forget it, Evan. I'm not thinking straight. You've certainly done enough for me."

"Let me take you home. I'd feel better knowing you are safe. Your parents have the cops after you; it's only a matter of time before they figure out where you are. Go back because you want to, not because they made you."

"Can I leave this hospital?"

"Yeah, they said you're free to go. I found your insurance card in your wallet and gave them that."

I yank off wires that are monitoring my pulse and swing my feet off the bed. Standing up requires a little more work since I'm still a bit woozy. Evan catches me as I almost fall.

"You stayed here all night?" I ask, resting in his arms.

"Sure did."

"Why? I've been so despicable. If you had treated me like that, I would've forgotten you existed."

"Good to know in the future. Look, this is some heavy shit you've been dealing with. You're just getting out your anger and frustration."

"Yeah, I tend to do that a lot."

He reaches over and grabs my clothes so I can change out of the hospital gown.

"I'll give you some privacy–"

I take off the gown. I want him to see me. His eyes linger and then quickly look away.

"I don't care."

I put back on the clothes I'd been wearing, not worrying about a bra and letting my tits swing. Evan gets the nurse and she clears me to check out. He'd driven my car over here so it's waiting in the parking lot. I slide into the shotgun seat and Evan takes the wheel. "All Apologies," blasts when he turns on the ignition, the song we'd been listening to when we'd found out Cobain died.

Neither of us knows how to react so we sit there breathing heavily. I don't need to screw away my pain anymore like before when I was acting naive, but I do want to be held. So I kiss him, our teeth clanging together, my bandage shifting around. We make out through "All Apologies," and then "Disarm" by the Pumpkins. When we pull away, my legs turn to jelly, even though I'm sitting.

"Let me take you home now." He goes to put the car in drive.

I put my hand over his. "No, not yet."

He squints into the distance like he's searching for the best response. "The rest of the band is going to this thing for Cobain by the Flag Pavilion. Maybe it'd be a good way to say goodbye."

I think of a world without Kurt and any more of his beautiful poetry. I'll have to hoard onto the songs I had of him like tiny nuggets of gold. I'll never get to shake his hand or tell him how much he meant to me, or have him write me a tune. We'd never sing together, or experience a kiss, or even a hug. He'd remain a stranger and over time he might vanish as I'd grow up and all my idols would lose their power and hold. The thought terrifies me because I know I'll never be as devoted to a musician as I am at sixteen, when music means everything without too many real-life responsibilities getting in the way.

Now that time has ended.

"Let's go to Flag Pavilion," I say.

21

• • • • •

Serve the Servants - Nirvana

In kick-ass grunge-rock style, we say adios to Kurt Cobain at a vigil with about five thousand kids who burst towards the massive water-spouting fountain by the Flag Pavilion. A loud-speaker system plays Nirvana's "Serve the Servants" while Evan and I watch a mosh pit descend on the fountain: teens plugging up the spigots, throwing up their middle fingers at the dusk, howling like wolves. Girls with mascara tears wear POLICE LINE DO NOT CROSS tape like beauty pageant sashes, the same tape that we saw fencing in Cobain's property two days earlier. Shirtless boys had dripped melted wax over self-made tattoos that spelled out k-u-r-t and moshed to the music, tossing each other into the widening arms of the pit below while others burn their flannel shirts, a rallying cry to how the media pigeonholed us. As their embers cut through the darkening sky, it makes a statement that we are more than just lazy fashion choices; we are a movement to be reckoned with.

Evan and I join the crowd that begins chanting "asshole, asshole," as if they are singing the end of "Smells Like Teen Spirit" and replacing "denial" with "asshole." We are angry that Kurt had chosen to leave us, not letting him off the hook so easily. Evan holds onto my hand, so we won't be separated as we navigate the mosh pit that sums up the stages of grief we all are experiencing. Anger exists in the sweaty cries and animalistic grappling of strangers. Sadness reflects on our faces, red with tears. Euphoria sneaks in as well because everyone is going through the same exact emotions at the same fucking time. We were lonely in our bedrooms with Nevermind spinning on our CD players. We're united at the Flag Pavilion, brought together by the only god on Earth I'd ever known.

Courtney Love appears, bedraggled and sleep-deprived, her dyed blonde hair a helmet around her head, her lips painted deep red. She has his suicide note in her shaking hands. The crowd stops moshing to pay attention to the Queen's speech about her King. As we step closer, the smell of rotten cotton candy mixes with wax and hippie incense. I plug up my nostrils.

"I don't really know what to say," Courtney Love begins, her voice filled with such sorrow that I instantly get a lump in my throat. "I feel the same way you guys do. If you guys don't think that I used to sit in his room, when he played guitar and sang, and feel so honored to be near him, you're crazy... Anyway, he left a note, it's more like a letter to the fuckin' editor. I don't know what happened. I mean it could've happened when he was forty. He always says he was gonna outlive everybody and be one hundred twenty. I'm not gonna read you all of the note cause it's none of the rest of your fuckin' business. But some of it is to you." She takes a deep breath. I imagine it's difficult for her to come out here and face the fans, but so necessary for our own grieving.

"And I don't really think it takes away his dignity to read this considering that it's addressed to most of you." She swallows another breath, shaking her head. "He's such an asshole. I want you all to say asshole really loud."

A chorus of "assholes" rises through the crowd. It feels good to let that word escape from my lips too.

"This note should be pretty easy to understand," she says, and I imagine Kurt's voice instead of hers filling up the atmosphere. "All the warnings from the Punk Rock 101 courses over the years since my first introduction to the, shall we say, ethics involved with independence and the embracement of your community has proven to be very true. I haven't felt the excitement of listening to, as well as creating, music, along with really writing something, for too many years now. I feel guilty beyond words about these things—for example, when we're backstage and the lights go out and the manic roar of the crowd begins, it doesn't affect me how it did for Freddie Mercury, who seemed to love and relish in the love and adoration from the crowd..." She turns to the audience, squeezing the note in her fist. "Well, Kurt, so fuckin' what? Then don't be a rock star, you asshole." Her mouth quivers and she returns to his last words. "...which is something I totally admire and envy. The fact is I can't fool you, any one of you. It simply isn't fair to you or me. The worst crime

I could think of would be to pull people off by faking it, pretending as if I'm having one hundred percent fun." She rolls her eyes. "No Kurt, the worst crime I can think of is for you to continue being a rock star when you fuckin' hate it. And just fuckin' stop." The pitch of her voice wavers as it becomes more difficult for her to continue. "Sometimes I feel as I should have a punch-in time-clock before I walk out on stage, I've tried everything within my power to appreciate it, and I do, believe me I do, but it's not enough. I appreciate the fact that I and we have affected and entertained a lot of people. I must be one of those narcissists who only appreciate things when they're alone, I'm too sensitive, I need to be slightly numb to regain the enthusiasm I once had as a child. On our last three tours I've had a much better appreciation of all the people I've known personally, and as fans of our music, but I still can't get out the frustration to gather the empathy I have for everybody. There's good in all of us and I simply love you people too much..." She shrugs her shoulders, giving up. "So why didn't you just fuckin' stay?" She wipes her running nose. "...so much that it makes me feel just too fucking sad. The sad, little, sensitive, unappreciated, Pisces, Jesus-man." She gives the note her middle finger. "Oh, shut up, bastard. Why don't you just enjoy it? I don't know. Then he goes on to say personal things to me that are none of your damn business, personal things to Frances that are none of your damn business." She chews on her finger, then continues: "I had it good, very good, and I'm grateful. But since the age of seven I've become hateful towards all humans in general. Only because it seems so easy for people to get along that have empathy…" She throws up her hands. "Empathy…? Only because I love and feel for people too much, I guess. Thank you all from the pit of my burning, nauseous stomach for your letters and concern during the last years. I'm too much of an erratic, moody, baby, and I don't have the passion anymore. Peace, love, empathy, Kurt Cobain." She can barely say his name, as if saying it out loud now fully means he's dead.

"And then there are some more personal things that are none of your damn business. And just remember, this is all bullshit and I'm laying in our bed, and I'm really sorry. And I feel the same way you do. I'm really sorry you guys. I don't know what I could have done. I wish I'd been here, and I wish I hadn't listened to other people, but I did. Every night I've been sleeping with his mother, and I wake up in the morning and I think it's him because their bodies are sort of the same. And I have to go now."

She leaves the stage, an ethereal spirit in white. We are connected, Courtney and I, bound by tragedy. I squeeze Evan's hand, his blue eyes dripping so many tears. I feel closer to him than ever before. I pull him away from the crowd until we are watching from a distance.

"We loved him," he says, by a tree. "But not like she did."

"We didn't know him." It hurts to admit this, but Cobain had always been nothing more than imagination. I'd built my own Cobain, just like Evan did along with everyone else. Our own robot rock star. Mine sang his poetry to me at night, surrounded by candles. Mine tasted like cola when we kissed. Mine got me pregnant once while on tour, and we had a baby that is just learning how to walk. Mine fed me uplifting choruses and allowed me to ease his demonic mind. Mine took me far from Laurel Canyon. Mine showed me how to live.

A circle of candles has been erected in the dirt by the tree. The breeze snuffed out the flames, so Evan takes out a lighter and we light them again.

"What do you want to tell him?" Evan asks, as the flames dance from the wind.

"You go first."

"All right. When I first picked up my guitar, Kurt, you were there to guide me. You were a patient teacher. You were a good friend. I miss you already, buddy."

He leans down and pinches one of the wicks until the flame goes out, then gestures for me to go next.

"Okay." I draw a heart in the dirt with the tip of my Doc Martens. The heart is lopsided, but I bet Kurt would've approved. "You took the place of someone I really loved when she left me." I get choked up, but Evan rubs my back in a soothing triangular motion. "I don't know what I would've done without your music and our late-night sessions when you were the only one I could talk to. I'll never forget how you held me up. I only wish I could've done the same for you."

I kneel and snuff out the rest of the candles. A thin layer of smoke curls from the wicks. Evan kisses me on the top of my head. The faint final chorus of "Serve the Servants" lets out its dying gasp as the crowd clears away from the Flag Pavilion to go mourn their savior alone.

• • •

We run into Lacey, Ed and Randy on our way back to my car. They haven't slept all night, passing from one vigil to the next filled with stories of other like-minded groupies who followed them on their bleary-eyed journey. We share the last cigarette Lacey has and stand in the mud shell-shocked, desperate for someone to speak.

"I think he would've been pleased with this," Lacey says. "As much as he could be pleased, I guess."

"He doesn't die," Ed says. "Don't you see? He gets to be immortal."

"Do you really think that twenty years from now people will still be playing his music?" Randy asks.

"Possibly more than if he lived," Evan says. "There's a mystique about dying young. Nothing worse for a rock star than to become old, fat, and irrelevant. Remember, he was twenty-seven just like Jim Morrison, Jimi Hendrix, Janis Joplin…"

I stay quiet, not wanting to talk about Kurt Cobain anymore. The funeral has ended and I don't want vultures picking apart the idea of him.

"What's next for you, girl?" Lacey asks, running her hand down my arm. "We're headed back to Eugene. Can only miss so many classes."

"Except for Randy of course because he's thirty!" Ed chuckles.

"It's my wealth of experience that keeps Grenade Bouquets afloat," Randy replies.

The two begin horsing around. I'm glad to see how quickly emotions could turn. It's their way of beginning to move on.

"When is your next gig?" I ask.

"We're gig-less for a minute," Lacey says. "Midterms are coming up so just some local Eugene haunts when Clarissa returns from Rome. But we'll make sure to go down to L.A. Will you be there?"

Evan catches my eye. I haven't definitively said I'm going home yet.

"Can you give us a sec, guys?" Evan asks.

"Sure thing," Lacey says. She kisses me close to my lips, an intimate farewell. "Please keep in touch, Nico."

"Thank you so much for letting me sing."

"No sweat. When you win your first Grammy, girl, make sure I'm in your speech."

"Of course! Since you'll be my manager too, I'll owe you for all my success."

Lacey grabs Ed and Randy by the back of their shirts to yank them away. "C'mon, Neanderthals, let the lovers say their goodbyes."

They begin to walk away, but then she reaches into her backpack to give me the hat we'd gotten at Salvation Army.

"You almost forgot this." She places it on my head. "It's the cherry on top of your whole ensemble."

I hold onto the brim and nod goodbye with a wink. They fade into the wild crowd pouring out into the streets.

"So you never answered her question," Evan says. "Are you headed back to L.A.?"

I think of the many possibilities that call to me beyond Seattle. I could avoid the reality of Kristen's death in Canada; I could head east on a road trip to New York until my Dad's gas card catches up with me. There are barely any songs left on the mixtape and no other bucket list items to complete. Continuing on would be nothing more than an excuse and an evil way to get back at my parents. I picture them hovering over the phone, waiting for a call with either good news or a tragic outcome like they faced with Kristen. I really believe that I'm not the same monster from when I left. I've learned from this experience. A semi-softened Nico would return. I'm able to think of other people besides myself. I can get over my anger and rage faster than I used to. I don't crave being messed out of my gourd like before, aware of the dangers that can happen now after hitting my rock bottom. I know now that tragedy can happen, but I don't have to let it define me anymore. So I need to face the music, however crappy it might be.

"I'm ready," I say. "Give me the keys."

Evan shakes his head. "Let me drive you all the way. We'll blast your mixtape and sing until our throats are raw. A proper send-off rather than just a lousy goodbye."

"Good." I smile from deep within. "I hate lousy goodbyes."

He grabs my chin and leaves a smacking kiss on my mouth. "There's those sparkling teeth of yours, Nico. I hadn't seen them in a while."

I hold onto the smile because it feels good to stretch my lips after they've been sagging downwards for so long.

22

• • • • •

Alive – Pearl Jam

On our way out of Seattle, Evan brings some cassette tapes since it's an eighteen-hour drive and eventually we'd get tired of Kristen's mixtape. He got Green Day's Kerplunk and their new album Dookie, which has been getting a lot of buzz. More punk than grunge, it's a new sound I'd been hearing, bored and rebellious rather than doomed. We listen to Kerplunk through the rest of Washington and Dookie on the way to Portland—going through my bucket list journey in reverse.

"You were really amazing on that stage, Nico."

I have my feet up on the dashboard, my muddy boots leaving brown clumps.

"I wish you could've seen it," he says. "Like, if I had a video of the show. You fucking glowed. Your sister would be very proud."

I take a bite of my lip, hang on for a sec. My mind is spinning, the highs and lows of my trip colliding.

"Yeah, I think she would have," I say. "Especially because I did something I loved so much. She always said that I needed focus. Like, the worst thing in the world was that I had no focus. But she just had too much focus. Like, she zapped up all the energy in the room and there was nothing much left over for me. Even with my parents, the little focus they gave us went to her. I know they were never being mean about it, it's like they didn't really want kids, you could tell, and I think Kristen was really good at pretending that wasn't the case and always being so busy with sports, and school, and, like being fucking perfect, and then there was me. Like, I'm funny, they'd tell me that sometimes, a jester performing for them, but then also this mopey little bitch who, like, sucked out the energy in the room in a really different way. If I wasn't acting terrible, who would even pay attention?"

"I paid attention," Evan says, his nostrils flaring. "And all those people at the show, they were paying attention. You can decide who you want to be."

"I just...don't want to get home and they turn this whole thing into me being the bad guy. Like, of course messed up Nico would run away. And I know that was a terrible thing to do, but I wouldn't have survived otherwise. And they need to fucking know that. They need to be around more for me. Like, shouldn't that be a big duh?"

"Part of the reason I don't go back to Idaho is that my dad kind of kicked me out."

I sniff up a giant snot ball. "Why?"

"Didn't join the Army. That's what Marvins do, we join. It's sick. Like, he fed off the war. And my mother is his back-up singer. Even after Chris returned."

"I'm glad you didn't have to go to Desert Storm."

"I don't even know what that war's all about."

"Kristen and I once," I say, feeling a tickle in my belly that causes me to laugh like a horse. I stop biting my lip as the memory shines bright. "I had this project to do for a theater class, and she agreed to help me. It was like a moment when I thought I'd be really into theater, but then I saw who I'd have to hang out with. Anyway, there was a blizzard so we couldn't leave. I decided to do an interpretive dance to that "Voices That Care" song where all the celebrities got together to stand tall and proud for the soldiers in Desert Storm. Kristen choreographed it and we practiced all freakin' day, like we were in the movie The Cutting Edge and I was Kate preparing for the Olympics in figure skating. It was the first time we spent more than five minutes with each other in forever, sans vacations. I went to sleep even humming the song, but before I passed the hell out—this is the real part of the story by the way—we realized a major, major thing.... We saw 90210 in two very different ways. And this was, like, huge. We knew we both watched it, but we each had separate TVs in our rooms, and since we barely hung out, neither of us would've even thought to suggest watching it together. Sometimes in passing we'd make a comment. Like, she surprisingly did not like Andrea Zuckerman, which was weird because she was basically a gorgeous Andrea Zuckerman, nothing against Andrea Zuckerman or anything. Or like we both agreed the best episode was when David Silver's kind of annoying friend Scott Scanlin shot himself with a gun when he was just messing around with it. And like Kristen loved Brandon, I loved Dylan, but we honestly liked both of them. The gigantic wedge between us was that she believed Dylan should be with Kelly, while I wanted Brenda, surly fucking Brenda that will cut a bitch with her eyes, and not beautiful blond Kelly, the poor rich girl with a cokehead mom. Like, I was not crying for Kelly. And so it became this thing, she'd call me Brenda and I'd call her Kelly, and it was just this little whatever, like we didn't even do it all the time... it just happened naturally. And to be honest, I would like her a drop more every time she called me Brenda, and I think she did it...." I stop, ready for the tears, but I realize I've emptied my well. "She did it because she knew I got a kick out of it, and like, that was gonna be our thing. We'd be middle-aged with kids and we'd call each other that and, like, our kids would have no freakin' clue what we are talking about. 90210 would be so uncool, and grunge as well, they'll be listening to something we so can't relate to, but this little piece of the past would just pop up every once and a while.

I think the hardest thing about losing her is that she's the person who's known me the longest, right? Like siblings always get to have that bond, and now I'm an...only child. It's so goddamn weird, ya-know? Like, I never prepared for that, it's just not fair. It's not FAIR. It's a raw deal, a really freaking raw-ass deal. And I'm pissed, Evan. I am fucking pissed and I don't know who to be pissed at so I'm pissed at everybody. And I'm having a hard time letting go of that. It's like I'm on this train, this fucking speeding train, and every time I think I can leap off, it goes faster, until one day it just flies off the rails."

"It did. You went off the rails, Nico. You literally

could've crashed and wound up in the hospital."

The sensation of snapping my head against the steering wheel pulses in my forehead.

"My friend Winter said I'd hit rock bottom."

"Winter's a smart girl."

"Winter's a lot of things."

"But you're alive."

I know there's a version of my story where I actually drove that car and destroyed my life. And then there's this other path with Evan driving me home like he is now.

"Yeah, I survived. I'm a survivor. I'm not gonna let that happen again," I say, placing my hand over my heart. "Swear to sweet baby Jesus and the manger."

"Ha, you remember my rejected band name."

He massages my shoulder, his fingers strong.

"You've come a long way, kid. I think you're gonna be okay."

A presence grabs my head and nods. Or maybe that presence has been me all along, the me I've been trying to steer back to.

"Thank you for telling me that story about your sister," Evan says. "I feel like I know her a little more now."

"She would've liked you. She'd want to give you a good bath, but after that, you guys would've gotten along."

"Shall we put in her mixtape?"

I take in a long breath through my nose.

"Yeah, let's do it."

We cue it up as Pearl Jam's "Alive" fills the car. Vedder isn't Cobain, but pretty great in his own right.

I only gave Winter shit about him to give her shit about something.

"Ready to roar, Nico?" Evan asks, drumming against the wheel.

I crank up the sound, the music blasting from the windows as we thrash our heads.

"Hey I-I-oh-oh-I'm still alive...."

23

• • • • •

When I Come Around – Green Day

When I see a sign that says we are nearing Ojai, I know I have to stop and see Aunt Carly. The numero uno reason being that I want her to call my parents and say I'm okay, thus minimizing the fallout potential of them going ballistic on my ass. But Ojai had also been the beginning of my journey, and I doubt my trip would've been the same had I not started there. Carly gave me the cojones to tackle my bucket list and for that, I'll forever be grateful.

"She has cats," I say to Evan. "Like, a lot of cats."

He shrugs. "Nothing wrong with that."

The day is ending when we arrive, the sun getting pinched by the mountains. She never locks her door, so we walk right in. Two bodyguard cats greet us, equally hissing and purring.

"She might be out on her back porch," I say, picking up a tabby cat and sliding open the glass door that leads to her backyard. The air smells of peaches and wine due to a massive tree on the property and an open bottle on her patio table. She sucks at a joint, nibbling the end.

"Nico," she says, waving me over as if she's been expecting us. "Who's this tall drink of water you've brought?"

"This is Evan."

She holds out her hand like a Victorian courtesan.

"My pleasure," she says. "Help yourself." She gestures toward the wine, almost knocking it over. Evan looks for glasses, but she shakes her head. "You can chug out of the bottle, we're all friends."

Evan takes a meaty chug, red wine lines dribbling down his chin.

"So...." Carly asks, drumming on her knees. "Tell me about your travels. Where'd you meet this one?"

"In Eugene, Oregon. But after Ojai, I went to San Luis Obispo. I climbed a mountain."

She narrows her eyes. "Aren't you the one afraid of heights?"

"Not anymore, I guess. Then I chained myself to a tree in Muir Woods and got arrested."

Evan passes the bottle to me. I don't really need to be drunk, but I take a swig anyway.

"Arrested?" Carly says, nodding as if she approved. "I remember the first time I stuck it to the man protesting the war in Vietnam. They brought out the tear gas for that one. You ever been tear-gassed?"

Neither of us answers.

"Anyway continue..."

"After San Fran, I met Evan in Eugene and then he let me sing in his band at a show in Portland."

Her face lit up. "Nico, you sang?"

"She was really fantastic," Evan chimes in.

"I always told this girl what a talent she had." She wraps a shawl around herself and grabs the bottle. "Come, the sun is fading away. It's getting cold. You'll stay the night."

We follow Carly back into her house. She makes up the couch so we both could sleep there.

"I have leftover Tofu Tetrazzini if you both want?"

She nukes her veggie delight and procures another bottle of wine for us to share. We eat on paper plates, and one of her cats joins us at the table as if it's eating too.

"My parents are looking for me," I say, when I'm almost finished. "They know I've run away."

Carly rubs her temples like she's trying to coax out her thoughts. "Your father will not be pleased."

"Has he called you to see if I'm here?"

She shakes her head. "We don't speak. He would never pick up the phone. I'm beneath him."

"Could you call just to say I'm all right? I think it'd be better if you spoke to them first."

"I'm not here to clean up your messes, Nico. You're getting old enough where you have to start learning how to do that for yourself."

She's right and I'm embarrassed for asking. I'm about to tell her that I'll call when she holds up her hand.

"Fine. But let me start sobering up," Carly says, rising to go make herself coffee. "I've been wanting to give them a piece of my mind too."

• • •

I listen outside of Carly's bedroom when she calls my Dad. I'd given her his new number, but his lady Annette answers and says he was staying at Luanne's while I was still missing. She sounds glad to know I'm okay. Carly then dials my home, and my mom picks up. There's a lot of Carly speaking to Mom like she's a slow child, telling her over and over I'm fine and that sometimes kids run away, especially due to all I'd gone through. She tells my mom to try and be supportive rather than angry. I overhear my mom tell her to pull her hippie nonsense out of her ass. Dad is even less forgiving when Carly gets on with him. By then, I pick up another line to fully listen to their exchange.

"Peter, she's an emotional wreck."

"This is coming from the biggest wreck I know."

"That's not fair."

"How many glasses of wine did you have today? How many cats do you have now?"

"She's hurting, Peter. Don't take your hatred of me out on her."

"I'm plenty angry with that kid on my own."

"Good, show some emotion. I'm sure Nico would like to see that more."

"What's that supposed to mean?"

"You are a cipher, Peter. You are humorless, and maybe your new woman likes that, but you neglected your child that's in my house now. This was a cry for help."

"I will not reward that kind of behavior."

"It's not about rewarding her, it's about acknowledging her feelings. Have you talked to her about Kristen?"

"We went to family therapy, it did nothing."

"Therapy is a lot of nonsense. Have you talked to her? Do you ever talk to her?"

Silence comes from Dad's end.

"When that girl gets home tomorrow, the first thing you need to do is hug her until she can't breathe. You can yell at her later but hug her first because that's what she needs the most."

"All right, Carly," he says, the tone of his voice ready to get rid of her.

"Thank you," Aunt Carly replies, and I hang up the phone.

I go back to her room and she retells me everything I'd already heard.

"I'm exhausted, Nico," she says, with an endless yawn. "So I'm headed to bed. Your father takes a lot out of me."

"You're a rad aunt."

Her sleepy eyes flutter. "I am a rad aunt." She lifts her head high and then pulls me close. "And don't do anything I would do with your tall blond boy." She nudges me in the ribs.

"We're zonked, Carly, we're just headed to bed too."

"Sure you are."

She closes the door. I crane my neck and see Evan on the couch. He's taken off his shirt and socks and is petting a black and white cat close to his chest. I'm unsure what I want to happen with him. Yeah, I could quietly do him, but in the morning we'd be saying goodbye. I know he isn't looking for a serious girlfriend who's still in high school, and even if he is, the distance would be too far to manage.

"You tickling some pussy over here?" I say, cackling

as I fall into the couch. The cat gives me a look that says, he is MINE.

"I think it's a boy cat," he says.

"Hey, I don't judge."

I ease in closer and the cat darts away in fright. Using this as an opportunity to make my move, I run my fingers up and down his leg.

"Nico..." He snaps his head back on the couch in frustration.

"Why do I feel like you're about to scold me?"

"Not scold, but I don't think we should...."

"Screw? My aunt won't care. She's halfway to Xanax dreamland."

I grab at his crotch, but he lifts my hand away like it's a dirty diaper.

"Ouch, never had that reaction before."

"Okay, we have sex and it's amazing, then what?" he asks.

"We do it again."

"When? You're a thirteen-hour drive away."

"But also just a two-hour flight."

"It's not realistic. Between classes and the band..."

"I know, I know." I snap my head back against the couch too. "I want you, though. What if we sleep together and it's so amazing that we're willing to do whatever it takes to make it work? I feel like I'll be a better person with you around. Less cuckoo."

"You don't need me to be better."

"I'd be dead without you. I would've remained a zombie in that flophouse."

He inspects my eyes. "Doesn't look like you want to eat brains anymore."

"Because you're here." I trace my finger around his nipple. He rests his nose on the top of my head.

"No, it's because you've come around, Nico. You're not that girl from two days ago, or from when you left home."

"I worry that she'll always be there, trying to wrestle out."

"So, we all have that. You don't think there isn't an Evan who wants to rage out of his skull? Every day is a battle."

I make a pouty face. "So, no sexy time tonight?"

"No sexy time, Brenda."

"Brenda wouldn't take no for an answer. She'd climb on top of Dylan and ride him all night till the rooster crows."

"You take the couch," he says, lying me down and tucking me in a quilt. "I'll sleep in the chair."

"You sure? I can make room."

He kisses me on the nose, and I know then we've solidified ourselves as great friends that wouldn't let fluids come between our bond. I decide I'd know him for a very long time. We'd be best buds in the retirement home.

"Thank you for everything, Evan. You really are one of the good ones."

He sits in a recliner and shifts until he's comfortable. "Right back at you, kid."

We shut off the lamps, the room pitch black except for a dozen yellow cat eyes blinking as nightlights.

• • •

In the morning, Evan and Aunt Carly are already on the porch drinking coffee when I wake, the sun creeping across the plains. I'm barefoot and chilly, cocooning myself in the floral quilt I'd slept in.

"Come join us," Carly says, waving me over with her arm covered in a shawl.

"Your aunt's telling me about her art. She wants to do portraits now."

"No more cats?"

"I'm looking for more vivid expressions out of my subjects," Carly says. "Could I paint you, Nico?"

"Yeah, I don't think I'm in the mood for that...."

She slaps her knee. "Not now, but you'll come back. We used to go years without seeing each other, and we're honestly so close by. If your mom and dad are grinding your gears and you feel like you need to get away, my door is unlocked and open any time."

"Wish I had an aunt like that," Evan says. "It's beautiful up here, Carly."

"This one's a keeper," she says, rising and heading inside. "I made fried egg and cheese rolls for the road. It's time for you to go, Nico."

We head out shortly after. The cats scurry outside to mewl goodbyes to us while Carly dramatically flaps her hands like we're headed off to war. Riding back to L.A., Evan and I don't speak much. I'm not ready to leave him and I hate that I can't tell whether he feels the same. I wonder if I should've pushed it further with him last night, or if that would've made things even more awkward today.

The hustle and bustle of L.A. startle me at first, even though it's only been about two weeks or so since I'd been gone. I'm not used to its plaguing traffic jams, and I get antsy the minute we hit a standstill. Evan tries to uplift my mood by putting back on some Green Day, but for once I'm not into hearing music.

Finally, we close in on Laurel Canyon and stop in front of my house.

"Home sweet home," he says.

I roll my eyes. "Far from." We get out of my car. "Oh shit, how are you gonna get back to Eugene?"

He sticks out his hitchhiking thumb. "I'll find my way. Don't worry your pretty head."

I burst out crying like a bloody fool. "I'm gonna really miss you, Evan. I want to act cool about it, but–"

"Hey, hey," he says, hugging me close. "This isn't goodbye. The Bouquets'll play a show in L.A. soon, promise."

"But it'll be different between us. I won't see you every day."

I can't believe I'm acting so melodramatic, but he just feels right, like I'm meant to be with him and he's worth fighting to stay together.

"Yeah, we won't see each other every day, but we can talk on the phone. We can write letters."

"Didn't I tell you I'm illiterate?"

He chuckles. "All right, the phone then. Whenever you need to hear my voice, never hesitate to give a ring."

"Don't say it if you don't mean it."

"I wouldn't." He puts my face in his hands; lets me gaze into his blue eyes one final time. "You're one of a kind, Nico."

"You say that to all the hot messes you know."

"No, just the former hot messes."

I lick my lips as the silence intensifies between us, and then he breaks it with a long, sweet kiss. I let all my worries and fears slip away, and the whole world becomes that kiss, so much so that when it ends and he's already gone, just a shadow hunching down the street with his hitchhiker's thumb directed at cars, I still kiss the air as if it's him, even after a car finally stops and takes him away.

Anyone passing would've thought I'd gone mad, but I'm long past madness now, finally circling back.

24

• • • • •

Release – Pearl Jam

As I turn the key and step inside, I brace myself. There will be a lot of yelling. A whole lot of crazy yelling. But I swear I'll hold my ground. Yeah, it was irresponsible to run away, but the 'rents need to understand that I had no other choice. They almost lost another daughter who's just starting to feel like she might be okay again.

Dad folds me into his chest before I even have a chance to speak. He'd been waiting at the door, probably watching me say goodbye to Evan. In that moment, I love him like I did when I was tiny and he was my hero. Mom soon joins in the hug, and we look like we are huddling over a football. Their hands touch, the most contact I've seen between them in a long time. We cry, for different reasons, but also for Kristen. We haven't done that before, avoiding one another like a disease. I hold on tight because I know this will only last a moment before the separation continues.

"Nico, we're very angry with you," Dad says. He isn't bawling like Mom, acting seriously even when he's sad. "You can't know what it did to us to have no clue where you were."

"I'm sorry," I say, to my boots.

"She's sorry," Mom says, throwing up her hands. "Young lady, you are a cruel child."

"I'm not a child!" I squeal, sounding exactly like a child.

Dad butts in to ease the tension. "I realize we've been neglecting you."

"No, you always neglected me. This is what you don't understand, Dad. Like, you were never around."

"Your father wasn't happy in this marriage," Mom says.

"What are you his defense attorney?" I snap.

"The police were looking for you, Nico. You could have been dead in some alleyway."

"I almost was."

Their faces go glum as I cover up my scar.

"Nico, what happened to your—"

"It's fine, it's fine. I just hit my head. It's no big."

"No big," Mom says with her hands on her hips, looking like she's fighting not to cry. I need a cigarette bad, but I know that won't help my case.

"You have a meeting with the school counselor tomorrow," she says. "They wouldn't even tell us if you're getting expelled!"

Mom has this vein that always pops when she yells, a lightning bolt shape on her temple. It throbs now like it's about to burst.

"They're not gonna expel me."

Dad crosses his arms. "You missed over two weeks of school."

"These two kids got in a knife fight the week before I left and they only got suspended."

I drag my duffel bag over to the couch. Sitting down, the couch smells like it always does, leathery with an after-note of cigars from all the ones Dad smoked.

"Aren't you even gonna ask about the life-changing experience I had?" I ask, running my hands through my hair. Do they even notice it is lavender? "Like, I am a different person now."

"In no way are you going to normalize what you did," Dad says. "You are grounded for a month."

"Don't be cliché, Dad. Buck the trend. Maybe you should be proud of me for being so independent."

"She thinks this is all a joke," Mom says, touching her vein as if it's a button she can push to calm down.

"No, I don't think this is a joke!" I yell. "I was spiraling, okay, and you two should've seen it and done something. But you were both distracted. You distracted yourselves, and I was dying."

Screw it, I think, taking out a cigarette and lighting it in front of them.

"Nico, you smoke?" Mom asks.

"Jesus Christ, Mom. I've been smoking since I was twelve. Do you have nostrils?" I inhale so hard my face scrunches up. "A few therapy sessions with that quack doctor who told me to draw my feelings after Kristen… It wasn't gonna fix what's happening to me." I start breaking down, tears like a geyser. I had put my own fears of dying aside for a while but now they've come roaring back.

"I think I'm going to die like Kristen," I say, the words quivering.

Mom sighs so deeply I can smell her breath.

"Nico, you're not going to die."

"I am this close to turning seventeen. Kristen was two days away and Dad's dad died at that age from the same thing."

"What are you talking about?" Dad asks.

"Didn't he?"

"He was young, but not seventeen and he caught pneumonia. Where did you ever get that idea?"

"Mom told me he died of a brain injury."

"It was a brain infection from pneumonia, I think. Right, Peter?"

"Anyway, what happened to Kristen was an isolated thing," he says. "It won't happen to you."

How have I been thinking this the whole time?

I shake my head, astounded. The room goes spinny. Maybe I honestly knew this all along. Once I feel like I can breathe, I suck in a final drag. I work to get my bearings and then stab out the cigarette. Who knows if I would've even made a bucket list if I didn't believe my ticket was destined to be punched too?

"You've always tended to hear what you want to hear," Mom says. "Ever since you were a little girl. So stubborn. Peter, do you remember the time she tried to convince us that the numbers go 1,2,4, 3, rather than 1,2,3,4?"

Dad chuckles, wiping his eyes. "She wouldn't go to bed."

"I knew my numbers. I was just messing with you both because I didn't want to go to bed."

"We knew that," Mom says. "Neither of us is as stupid as you think."

I've been keeping my anxiety in my hunched shoulders. I release them along with a woosah sound that I'd heard Aunt Carly do.

"I really thought I was gonna die," I say.

"Peter, she's avoiding what she's done."

"I'm aware of that, Luanne."

"I had a bucket list," I say, whipping it out of the duffel bag. I'm about to hand it to them and then hesitate, but I honestly want them to know I haven't been just dicking around. "Like fears I had…I climbed a mountain and surfed. Like, can you picture Nico in nature?"

Mom peruses the bucket list as if it's a court document. She passes it to Dad.

"Kiss a boy you really like?" he questions, frowning.

"Yeah, I did that too. The one who drove me home from Seattle. We were there because I was gonna sing in his band at a paid show! I sang in Portland and it caused the lights to go out, but then people came back and moshed to my songs."

"Mos-hed?" Mom asks, spacing out the word, no clue what it meant.

"Yeah, like, they were super into it. I've always been afraid to sing in front of an audience, but it's, like, what I'm born to do. I don't want to do anything else!"

I'm so jazzed and I need them to see my excitement. Maybe I'm not school smart, but I have passions too, even if they're more alternative.

"What you're not seeming to get is how disappointed we are with you," Dad says, exhausted, probably wishing he's about to tear into a pile of financial documents rather than my ass. "You have no respect for us."

"Because you are both living like you're at some suburban key party. You with our neighbor and you with some French coquette." I point at them both in case they didn't realize who is who.

"Peter, let's tell her," Mom says, nodding for Dad to agree.

"Nico, your mother and I haven't been together for a while," he says. "That's why I was rarely home. We were going to tell you and Kristen..."

"Jesus Christ!" I turn to Mom. "And were you with Weirdo Ferguson all along?"

"Please don't call him that..."

"Truth bombs!" I order. "Right now! How long was this masquerade going on?"

"I've been seeing Annette for about five years," Dad says.

I smack my forehead. "Since I was eleven, like, what the hell?"

"Your mother and I didn't want to split up the family."

"And you and...Ferguson?"

"About two years," Mom replies. "You're too young to understand this but sometimes adults need different things from one another. Your father and I weren't fulfilling each other."

"So why didn't you just divorce? Like, if I hated someone, I wouldn't make their breakfast every morning."

"We co-existed like this for a while," Dad says, "and it worked."

"No, it gave you both reasons to be away from home, and me, and Krist.... She always made excuses for you both, like, she couldn't see how selfish the two of you were. But I knew."

"I won't argue with that," Dad says. "We were neglectful."

"I can think of better adjectives than that."

"But Nico, you are difficult as well. You can sometimes just be so moody. You suck the life out of things. Don't you see that?"

I stare at him in awe that he could be so hurtful, but it's true. I've referred to myself in the same way.

"I'm glad to hear you got to sing," he says.

Mom jerks her head in confusion. "Peter!"

"We always said she's directionless, Luanne. Maybe this is what she needs."

"So, you're going to sing in some band?" Mom asks. "Drop out of school?"

"You said they might expel me anyway."

"This is what I mean, Peter, her smart mouth. Everything is hilarious to you."

I leap up and scream in her face so loud her hair blows back.

"Nothing is hilarious! Everything has been shit. Kristen fucking died and nobody even talks about her. It's like we had to pretend she didn't exist."

"Nico stop," Dad says.

"No, you need to hear this. I miss her and no one knew her like the three of us did so when I'd talk about her to Winter or Jeremy or like a school counselor or a stranger, they are sad for me, but they don't miss her like I do. It hurts. It's this, like, physical pain that I always carry around."

"We have that too," Dad says, his arm around my

neck holding me back. Apparently, I was lunging at Mom. "And it will never go away." He looks at Mom who sighs again.

"I tried what I can to avoid talking about it...about her," Mom says. "To avoid the pain. I don't know. I don't have the answers. Nobody tells you how to deal with something like this."

"Music has like saved me," I say. "On this trip listening to certain songs made it like Kristen was with me."

Mom walks over and loops a fried strand of my lavender hair around my ear.

"Nico," she says, sweetly. "How did it feel when you sang?"

"I...left my body. I had a break. That's what I'm trying to say. I didn't want to slit my wrists and curl into a bloody ball for once. I'd made a mixtape for Kristen for her birthday that I obviously never got to give to her. And so, I took this tape and played it the whole time I was traveling, like I was doing this bucket list for her. Things I've always wanted to do, but that she probably wanted to do too. Because she was so driven and had no time for fun once she hit high school. It was all for her."

Mom hugs me and we stay like that for a moment. I feel her heavy breaths against my chest and rest my chin on her shoulder. I throw my arms around her too and sob, emptying myself completely.

"And then Kurt Cobain died! Like, have you seen my room? This was the man I wanted to marry. And he just gave up."

"We found out you might have gone to Seattle,"

Dad says.

"We went to a vigil for him and like, five thousand kids were there, everyone loved him so. And they were sad but fucking damaged from it too. Like, he took the easy way out."

"He did," Dad agrees.

"You don't have to worry about me slitting my wrists or even running away again."

"Because we're gonna lock you in your room." He wipes away my tears with his thumbs. "You are grounded for a month."

"Yeah, that's totally fair," I say, figuring I'll give them some satisfaction in scolding me.

Mom brushes my hair. "We'll talk about your living arrangements later."

"I really want to just go to my room now. Am I done with being punished?" I smack the back of my hand. "Bad Nico. Bad Nico."

"We have to have a serious talk about what you did and all the consequences," Dad says. "But for now, yes, go to your room."

I sling the duffel bag over my shoulder and stand at the foot of the stairs.

"I really am sorry," I say, truly feeling terrible and needing them to know this. "I didn't run away to hurt you. I mean, maybe a little, but I really just needed, like, a break from it all. And now, I need a massive nap."

They both wave me away, just as wiped out from the ordeal. It's nice to see them united, even if I'm the target, even if it's for a short amount of time. I take in their unified image because I doubt I'll ever see them together like this again.

• • •

Upstairs, my room seems smaller. A tiny, cluttered alcove with too many Cobains staring at me. Angry Cobain. Wailing Cobain. Sad Cobain. Grinning Cobain. I wonder if it'd be cliché to tear down all my Nirvana posters, or if I'd be jumping the gun and regret it instantly. I zip open the duffel and take out a stack of Polaroids held together by rubber bands. Gregg with three g's and I at Ojai Meadows Preserve. I laugh about thinking he looked like Matt Dillon till I found out what a tool he was. Pismo Beach and the gnarly waves. Another one of Stephen and I on the mountain, his winning smile stealing the entire picture. He was so sweet. A picture of the tree I'd chained myself to, still in disbelief that Stephen came all the way to SF to bail me out when I was arrested. A snapshot of the wine bottle I stole on the gas station bathroom sink with some Manic Panic Hair Dye. Me singing "Silent All These Years" at the open mic, my eyes off in another world. There are multiple pictures of the Grenade Bouquets. Lacey and I trying on hats at the Salvation Army in Eugene. Evan, Randy and Ed posing like they are on the cover of Rolling Stone. Us at Flag Pavillion as hundreds of Cobain mourners poured into the fountain. And Courtney Love, disheveled and raw, as she faced Kurt's fans two days after his suicide. Then there's definitely a few of Evan. Evan alone in the passenger's side of my car, his blond hair tossed by the wind, squinting so much he looks asleep. Evan again in Aunt Carly's house with a black and white cat in his lap.

I tack them all up on a board over my desk.

I place the one of me and Kristen at Big Sur dead center.

My wild and hella insane journey.

That isn't over yet.

25

• • • • •

Come Down - Bush

After a super necessary shower and a nap, I wait until my parents go to bed and sneak out to see Winter. In case they wake up, I leave a note telling them where I'm going, that I'm definitely not running away again, and that my grounding can start tomorrow. When I get there, Edina is up, her orange pom pom hair in pigtails, Janis Joplin faintly playing on the record player.

"You're home," Edina says. I can't tell if she is happy or pissed. I had gotten her into trouble with my stunt.

"I'm real sorry, Ed–"

She brushes it away. I hadn't even noticed a joint in her hand, practically sucked down to the nub.

"How was the trip?" she asks, leaning in close, her eyes a flutter.

"It was…amazing."

"Then that's all I need to hear." She sizes me up. "You're looking good, Nico. The energy surrounding you is colorful. Before you left, it was cloudy."

"My energy?"

"We all have auras," she says, biting down on the joint for one last drag. "Yours is sometimes a difficult one to visualize, but tonight, honey, it's shining."

She leaves a lipstick kiss on my cheek and goes over to a record player to change the song.

"I'm really sorry about your idol," she says, caressing the record player sleeve of Joplin with purple sunglasses. "You know Janis was twenty-seven too. I remember where I was when she died, a freshman at high school. Heroin overdose. Tragic. She had so much more to offer the world. My friend Kathleen and I cried in a stall in the loo. The whole school was silent, like we'd all known her. I wrote a poem to her in heaven that night. I was so young."

"Yeah, I heard they were the same age," I say, surprised that I'm not getting choked up like before, Kurt's death no longer a shock.

"Maybe they're jamming in a band right now with God at the drums? I imagine they would've gotten along." She shakes her head. "You'll never forget your first idol's death."

I have nothing to say to that.

"I'm gonna go see Winter."

Edina changes the song and I hear the beginning of "Piece of My Heart" until I'm too far away to make it out anymore.

At Winter's door, Bush's Sixteen Stone plays. Bush has a glossier sound than most of the grunge bands I like, as if their music is being prepped to be a soundtrack for a movie starring Marky Mark.

I knock as I enter. Winter sits cross-legged on her

bed, a cigarette hanging out of one side of her mouth, a small bottle of vodka in her lap. She wears an extra-large sweatshirt that hangs off her shoulder, and she'd taken the cornrows out of her hair.

"Nico?" she says, as the cigarette slips from her lips. She quickly puts it out before it lights up her comforter.

"The one and only," I say, and do a ta-dah dance.

She flings her arms out and pulls me into her bosom, kissing the top of my head like a mama bear.

"Holy hell, girl. Did you parents shit a Mack Truck when you got home?"

"Yeah, they went ape on me. But were surprisingly cool about it too. I'm grounded for a month, though."

"Whatever, you'll just sneak out."

"Yeah…." I quietly say.

She sits up on her knees and takes down a jewelry box from a top shelf. Her box o' drugs.

"Let's puff and do shots, bitch. We have mucho to catch up on."

She glugs from the bottle and packs a fat bowl and then rubs her hands together. "Bottoms up, sunshine."

She tokes as her body tingles. I have a vision of her doing this five years from now, ten, fifteen, a jaded housewife waiting into the late hours for her suit n' tie husband to come home and relieve her boredom.

"Nico, why are you staring at me like that?"

She passes over the swirly glass pipe.

"Yeah, I'm good, Winter."

"No, you're entirely too sober for us to catch up." She pushes the pipe back at me.

"I said I'm good."

"Please don't tell me that this new Nico who walked

into my room is a lame bitch."

"I have a meeting with the school counselor tomorrow. I don't even know if they're gonna kick me out or what."

"You're not getting kicked out. Remember those two idiots who got in the knife fight? They're back at school."

"I know, I know."

"So you have zero excuses. Now toke!"

I turn away so I don't have to look at her. Over her desk she has a corkboard full of Polaroids like I do—except in all of hers she appears bombed out of her mind.

"Can you remember the last time we had fun sober?" I ask. When I finally look back, she's taking another dragon puff.

"What?"

"Like, all the fun we have centers around getting messed up."

"So? We're sixteen. We have nada responsibilities."

"Maybe I want responsibility."

Winter folds her arms. "Have you gone all Jesus on me?"

"No. Why would you say that?"

"You told me about the Jesus-loving boy who bailed you out of jail."

"I'm not in love with him so don't worry about me becoming a missionary or anything. Besides, I met a guy after him."

Winter squeals and thrashes her head. She cranks up her stereo, Bush's "Come Down" rocking the walls.

"Give me the deets."

"He plays in a band. The one I sang in."

"Hot. What does he look like?"

"Like a baby Kurt Cobain."

"Maybe he's his soul reincarnated? Also, I didn't want to bring up K.C."

"So, I went to his vigil in Seattle," I say, leaping on the bed and holding onto her hands that are so sweaty. "We heard Courtney Love speak."

"I saw that on MTV."

"Like five thousand kids were there and then we all screamed asshole because Cobain was such an asshole for leaving us like that."

"I don't know what I'd do if Vedder killed himself," Winter says. She spins around and kisses his poster. "You're so much stronger than me, Nico."

"I know I am."

"Don't sound so confident," she says, with a half-hearted laugh. "You travel for like two weeks on your dad's gas card and think you know everything?" Her handshakes as she tries to relight her cigarette.

"It's the filter end."

"I know that!" She flips it around. "At least you have a father who semi-cares. Mine couldn't get away from me fast enough."

"But Edina is like a mom and a dad."

"Edina is certainly a character," Winter says. "But more like a friend than an actual mom. Not that I'm complaining."

"Of course not."

"When your parents came over trying to find out where you were, they were, like, so angry. It was kinda sweet. If I ran away, Edina would be cheering at my departure. She even tried to compare me to you. 'Nico is such a trendsetter.' That's exactly what she said."

"Really?"

Winter points her finger in my face. "Yeah, well it was my idea anyway. Even people at school have been talking about you these past two weeks."

I pick at my nails. "What were they saying?"

Winter takes another swig of vodka. "Like you are some innovator. Like no one had ever run away before."

"You could've come."

"And once again, Nico, everything is all about you again. People asking where you were now. And then once the cops started to look, forget it. You were more popular in your absence than you or I ever were normally."

"That isn't why I did it!" I snap, getting pissed at Winter. Everything is not all about me, she always makes it about her.

"I know you had your reasons." She grabs my shoulders, widening her eyes to show me her spider web bloodshot veins. "But if I ran away, everyone would just think it was a cry for attention."

"You told me I needed to hit rock bottom and I did, Winter. I took a pill I shouldn't have and woke up in the hospital."

I haven't needed the bandage since I'd left Seattle. I'd covered up the scar with a hefty dose of make-up, but it's still visible.

Winter runs her finger across my forehead. "Gnarly."

"I wanted to die."

"So I wanted to die yesterday, get in line."

"Why?"

She hugs herself tightly. "I was thinking about my child."

Right, Winter told me she'd gotten an abortion before I left.

"I'm sorry, Winter." I hug her as well and wipe her emerging tears.

"Maybe I wanted to keep it, I don't know. But Edina, she put her foot down about refusing to help raise it. She doesn't want to be a grandmother yet."

"Are you really ready to be a mother?"

She sniffs. "No. I don't know. But for, like, one second, I wondered if having a kid might just chill me out or something."

"Look, I'm not pretending I'm about to become a saint. But it's a school night, do you really need to drink and smoke so much?"

"I don't know what else to do."

"Let's try without it, just for a week, like to give our lungs and liver a break. Are you in?"

"Am I gonna remember this in the morning?"

I find a potted plant on her dresser, pick up a black marker, and write NO POT on the outside and NO DRINK on the bottle of vodka.

"Nico, you so crazy."

"I missed you, Wint."

Winter puckers her lips for a kiss and I give a quick peck. She pushes aside the sheets and I crawl inside her warm bed, clutching her tightly.

"Tell me about the rest of your amazing jaunt," Winter says. "Have you come down from it all yet?"

"Hardly."

"Give me the highlights, Nic Nic."

"Singing in Portland definitely. It's what I want to do for the rest of my life."

"Sing to me now. Let me hear those dope pipes."

Bush's "Come Down" still plays from her stereo so I wait until I recognize the chorus.

"I don't wanna come down from this cloud.

It's taken me all this time to find out what I need."

I repeat it over and over.

"Did you find out what you need?"

I swallow, really thinking about Winter's question before I answer.

"I'm getting there."

"Maybe you're right...." she says, twisting a strand of white hair around her finger.

"What about?"

"Going so hard all the time. I use the excuse that I get messed up because I'm bored, but we live in L.A. There's, like, so much to do."

"I'm up for anything on your bucket list, Wint," I say, and gave a rat-tat-tat laugh.

"Maybe I should make one too. What was on yours again?"

"Singing in front of a crowd, of course. Learning guitar, surfing, climbing a mountain and facing my fear of heights. And kissing a boy I really like."

"So, this Kurt Cobain-looking motherfucker that you fell for, what's his name?"

"Evan."

"Are you gonna see young Evan again?"

"Old Evan. He's a freshman at the University of Oregon."

"Ooooohhhh, yeah high school boys don't know how to use their dicks right anyway. It's all pump, pump, pump, adios. Just ask that piece of garbage, Vince, who I went to Pearl Jam with."

"You guys aren't hanging out anymore?"

"He suggested a threesome with this Chihuahua-looking loser he knows. When I told him no, he called me a tease. Like, you can call Winter a lot of things, but she ain't a tease, she has some kind of standards."

"I'm sorry he sucks."

"So, will you see this Evan again?"

I glance out of the window, as if Evan is watching. By now he's probably halfway back to Eugene. And next week, I don't know if he'll be thinking about me as much, or the week after, until eventually his ex Clarissa returns from Italy or another girl captures his interest.

"He lives so far away."

"Yeah, distance definitely doesn't make the heart grow fonder. No worries. We'll find you another dick here."

"I'm not looking for just a dick."

"Yeah, we're getting too old for that wham, bam kind of love. We're ladies now and should be after substance."

"To substance," I say, and we make a pinky promise.

I wait a long time until Winter comes down from her high and falls asleep before I leave. As I lean over to turn out her lamp, I see how stressed she looks while sleeping. Grinding her teeth. Grill marks across her forehead in the form of worry lines. I know I have to watch out for her hitting rock bottom too and encourage her own bucket list to help pick up her sorrows.

"I love you, Wint."

I kiss her worried forehead that's blasted with sweat. I change the CD to Vs. because I know Eddie Vedder can cull her nightmares like no one else. I pray he'll never follow in the same path as Cobain.

But I have faith in Vedder living a long life. Someone needs to preserve my beautiful grunge music. The torch has been firmly passed to him to keep it lit for all the tortured souls wading through the darkness.

Like Winter is.

And I used to be.

26

• • • • •

Everybody Hurts – R.E.M.

Ms. Poole, the school counselor is known as Lady Chris Farley because she's a dead ringer for the comedian, right down to the bowl haircut. She likes angels so her office is smattered with them, as if they might help to guide any wayward youth who require her services. Today she wears pleated khaki pants with a lime green sweater and penny loafers. Jesus Christ. She has a bagged lunch sitting on her desk that's probably full of La Yogurt and a Polly-O String Cheese.

"So…Nico." She folds her sausage fingers together, switching from a chirpy tone to more serious. "Is what you did a cry for help?"

I glance at a cardboard angel that's weeping. The only reason I cry now is that I know it'll take a while to maneuver my way out of this mess.

"Is it because of what happened to your sister?"

Her own eyes start welling up, and I think, Jeez, am I really gonna have to comfort her?

"I'm fine now."

"Sometimes we bottle things up," she says, her tongue picking at a gap in her teeth. "And then. Boom."

"Yeah, the bottle exploded but all is well with the state of Nico again."

She picks up my file like she hasn't already perused it a million times.

"What do you want from your future?"

"Does this mean I'm not getting expelled?"

"No sweetie, but I look at your grade point average and I do not like what I see."

"I want to be a singer."

"That's fine," she says, tapping a pencil against her three chins. I can tell she doesn't approve. "What if that doesn't pan out? Don't you want to consider college as a fallback?"

"Four more years of tests and classes?" I squawk. "No, thank you."

"You could think of a music school where you take classes you'd be interested in."

"That exists?"

"There are plenty around the country. My niece goes to the Berklee School of Music in Boston. They have an exceptional program."

"Boston?"

My knowledge of Boston is a bunch of red-faced people braving blizzards who speak in weird accents.

"There are ones in California too."

God, Lady Chris Farley, why can't you just leave me alone?

I stare at her, this middle-aged woman with a kid's haircut. She thinks she does such wonderful things for the students every day by helping them find their path. But really, I can only think about what a major makeover she needs.

And then, I have an image of Stephen, conferring with one of the angels taped up to Ms. Poole's wall.

"Don't judge her," Stephen says, his smile blinding white. "What Would Stephen Do?"

"Okay," I say, telling my brain to give this poor creature a chance. "Music school might just be what I need."

"Oh, good," Ms. Poole replies, tickled by my response. I can see a shiver pass across her flesh. "Good, good, good."

She passes me over a brochure for the Berklee School of Music along with the California College of Music in Pasadena.

"I can look into other ones for you," Ms. Poole says.

"Please do."

I get ready to leave, but her sausage fingers grip my wrist.

"If you ever need someone to talk to, Nico.... Running away is not the answer. Everybody hurts. Do you understand?" She reaches into what I think is her bag of lunch and pulls out a cassette tape of R.E.M.'s Automatic for the People. "A colleague of mine told me about this band called Rem."

"You mean R.E.M."

"What's that, love?"

Oh well, whatever, never mind.

"Anyway, they have a song called 'Everybody Hurts'. And what that means is that everybody goes through pain in their life, which is why pain is universal. If you think you are the only one suffering, someone else is likely suffering too. You are not alone."

"I am not alone," I repeat, so she'll let go of my freaking wrist already.

"Listen to it, and if you ever feel like things are getting too hard..."

"I'll come right to you...Ms. Poole."

I almost say Lady Chris Farley, glad that I catch myself.

"You take care now, Nico."

When she lets go, white finger marks appear around my wrist. Ms. Poole was not playing around. I give her a curtsey, so she can see I'm well behaved and then book it out of there like I'm about to piss my jorts.

I go to my locker and pop in headphones. R.E.M. is not my cup of tea, a little too whiny for my tastes and Michael Stipe doesn't ooze sex appeal; but I don't hate them. Like, if someone is super into R.E.M., I wouldn't bash their skull. They aren't Ace of Motherfucking Base.

I chuckle at that.

At our Jewish cousin's Deborah's bat-mitzvah, Kristen and I made a music video to R.E.M.'s "Stand." I was mortified because I was twelve and everything mortified me. Kristen loooooved it and wanted to watch the video over and over so one day I climbed up to our roof and tossed it down the chimney to a roaring fire below. God, what I dick I was.

I fast-forward until "Everybody Hurts" comes up with its maudlin crooning. Michael Stipe really does have a beautiful voice, though. Haunting and mysterious. He's no Cobain, or even Vedder, but not everyone set out to be. I watch my fellow students passing by, most of whom I'd never bothered to pay much attention to. Those who played the high school popularity game baffled me, since I'd never want to be celebrated in this petri dish. Take Morgan Kaylens, an ice queen with an ice skaters body and vicious little teeth that she uses to chew up all of her hangers-on. Her flock worships her tiny feet, but she always appears as if she's about to vomit, which she probably is. Michael Stipe keeps crooning, and I have to admit that I'd never realized how miserable perfect Morgan Kaylens might be. At my worst, I could not stick a finger down my throat. I love cake too much to disrespect it like that. Or Lance Brayson, quarterback of the football team, who is cute in a meathead way, but stupid on a major level. Like, he'll be dumb for the rest of his life and probably goes home and cries dumb tears some days because he's too clueless to understand what everyone is saying around him all the time.

Or Winter and Jeremy. I spy them by Winter's locker down the hall. Winter looks cracked out and I wonder if she's toked before class, even though she promised me not to touch pot or alcohol for a week. Winter fucking hurt. And Jeremy too. He once told me of a botched suicide attempt where he took a bunch of his mom's pills only to realize they were Advil and just gave him a bad stomachache and the shits for days. He fucking hurts because he gets picked on at school on a bad level sometimes by anyone but Winter and me.

"Bee-yotch!" I hear him screech from down the hallway. He moonwalks over to me. Jeremy can do a killer Michael Jackson. He won a talent show for it when he was ten or something.

He almost knocks me over with a strangling hug. Winter follows close by, pushing her white bangs over her eyes.

"Girl, we missed your juicy ass," he says, shaking his own bony one. "Like, there aren't enough juicy asses around here to keep things interesting."

Morgan Kaylens saunters by with her gaggle of other waifs and Jeremy gestures at them to make his point clear.

"Winter filled me in on some of your runaway stories, but I want to hear it from the duck's lips," he says, licking at his own like he has cottonmouth. Yep, the two of them had gotten blasted at sunrise.

"It was a pretty wild experience," I say, but I don't really feel like putting what I'd been through into words. It was my journey, not for the masses. I'd just give him a little nugget.

"I sang for real at this venue in Portland with a band!"

I look for a reaction, but Jeremy and Winter are obsessing over some girl with toilet paper stuck to her shoe.

"Hello," I say, waving in front of them.

They giggle and hug each other.

"Meet any boys?" Jeremy asks, his tongue pressing against his cheek in mock-fellatio.

"Yeah, this really cool guy," I say, trying not to be annoyed that they weren't paying attention to the major boast I had about singing. "Looks like a young K.C."

"I know you like 'em skinny and unwashed," he says. "Oh shit, I have to tell you about Asa Levenfeld, my shotgunning boy!"

"Oh right. Did you guys make-out for real?"

"Yes, bitch, BUT, and this but is even bigger than yours. This but has to do with when we were high out of our gourds after a pretty heavy tonguing session and he brings up the fact that his mother still breastfed him up until he was in first grade. Like, what the hell?"

"That's gross."

"Uh, it killed the mood. Forever! Now he follows me around like a sad little puppy, and I tell him, go get your mother's milk cause you ain't getting mine."

He snaps his fingers in a Z formation.

"Anyway, I'm convinced I'm not meeting the love of my life in these corroded walls. We have to go to this new club Debauchery that I heard about."

"Okay," I say, croaking on the word.

"But like, we have to get shit from Raoul before. Oh yeah, Raoul is our new pot guy ever since Sammy got arrested."

"So much has changed," I say, being sarcastic but Jeremy doesn't pick up on it.

"Not as much as this hair," he says, fingering one of my split ends. "Dig the lavender, Nico Rico Suave, makes you look less butch."

"You're quiet," I say to Winter, who's still fixing her bangs so they cover her eyes.

"DoyouhaveVisine?" she mumbles to Jeremy, who digs into his jeans jacket and whips out a tiny bottle.

"Don't say I never give you anything," he says.

She leans back against a locker and plops in a few drops.

"So, I'm not getting expelled," I say. "Ms. Poole just

gave me an R.E.M. tape and some college brochures for music schools."

"God, I'd rather be plowed with a splintered broom handle than be here today," Winter says, to no one in particular. "I think we're gonna skip."

She beckons me with her index finger.

"No...I can't."

"Really Nico?" she whines, grabbing Jeremy by the arm and pulling him close until they fuse into one being with two bobbleheads.

"I just missed over two weeks!"

"Right, better get cracking on those college applications."

"Why are you acting so bitchy, Winter?"

"Ruh roh," Jeremy says, mimicking Scooby Doo.

"I'm bitchy because I can tell how you're looking at me," Winter snarls.

"And how is that?"

"Like you're superior. Because we got blasted before we entered this god-awful building of phonies, and you come off like you're better than us all of a sudden."

"I never said I was."

"Why couldn't I have a dead sister so I could take a vacation?" Winter yelps, dashing out of school, the sleeve of her giant sweatshirt mopping up her leaking eyes.

"She didn't mean that," Jeremy says, rubbing my shoulders.

I bite the edge of my lip as a way of keeping my shit together.

"Yeah, she did."

Winter was acting just like I had before I took off,

lashing out at everyone because I was so miserable.

I bolt out of school after her, Jeremy close behind. Winter is by the basketball courts trying to light a cigarette, but the wind keeps betraying her. Finally, she tosses her lighter and the cigarette as well.

"Hey," I shout. "Hey! You don't get to say something like that and just run away."

"You said whatever you felt and then ran away."

"Fine, what do you really want to say to me?"

"We were messes...together, don't you see?"

"So, you're upset that I've been doing better? That's crazy, Winter. You encouraged me to go so I could get over Kristen..."

I stop and take in a swell of breath.

"Like, I don't feel her death in the pit of my stomach anymore. Why would you want to take that away from me?"

Jeremy catches up, his eyes flitting between Winter and me trying to gauge the situation.

"Are the claws still out?" he asks, but we both ignore him.

"If you're not a trainwreck anymore," Winter says, seething, "then where does that leave me?"

"You don't have to be a trainwreck either."

"I've always been one, you only decided to join me a few years ago. I have depression, Nico, and like Edina doesn't believe in meds. I could take a suppository of psychedelics and she wouldn't blink, but god-forbid I'm allowed some anti-depressants. So I live with it, okay?"

"I didn't know that," I say, feeling very small.

"Yeah, I don't make it my business to share."

"I didn't know that either," Jeremy says, massaging her arm. "I can get you some from Raoul probably."

"That's a real friend!" Winter screeches.

"I've always been a real friend to you just like you have been to me. You once told me we're closer than sisters."

"I can already figure out what I'll become to you, Nico. Crazy Winter. Good for a laugh, but ultimately nothing more than time suckage."

"I'd never think that."

"You already do. Going to class? What the hell? And writing NO POT on my plant. Who do you think you are, my sponsor?"

"No, I mean... You saw when I needed help and now..."

"Oh wow, Nico, thank you so much, wise sage."

"Girls, why don't we just do something fun now that Nico's back?" Jeremy says, grinning. "Put the talons away."

"I don't think I'm superior," I say, brushing her bangs away from her eyes because I hate that look on her. "I'm sorry if I made you feel that way."

"I'm not ready to not be a trainwreck," she says.

"Okay, you don't have to become valedictorian tomorrow."

"So like, don't push it with me. All right? Or we'll have problems."

"Loud and clear, Winter."

"You were ready, Nico. I'm not. I need you to understand that."

"Scout's honor."

"Good."

She shakes all the negativity out of her and emerges a different Winter.

"Good," Jeremy says, putting his arms around our shoulders and pulling us into his armpits.

"Are you wearing perfume?" I ask him.

"Just a splash of my mother's White Diamonds," he says, and then puts on his Liz Taylor voice. "These have always brought me luck."

"You are the biggest disaster," Winter says, weaseling out from under his arms. She starts cracking up. "Jesus, it's impossible to stay upset with our court jester Jeremy around."

I kiss Winter on the cheek. "I truly love you, Winter. I'm not trying to change you."

She shrugs her shoulders. "I'm glad my runaway suggestion turned out great."

Everybody Hurts, I want to tell her, but wisely keep quiet.

We hear the bell faintly ring.

"So I suppose you want to head to class?" Winter says.

"I think Lady Chris Farley will have my head if I don't," I reply. "They really were considering expelling me."

I'm lying because I know both of them aren't ready to hear the truth about how I feel about their antics. It's like, I couldn't really see them and how I'd been until I spent enough time away.

"All right," Winter sighs. "What about you, Jer Jer? Shall we do an impromptu trip to the Viper Room?"

"I got a bottle of Absolut in my bag."

"Aces," Winter says, clicking her tongue.

"Say hi to River for me," I say, giving her a hug.

"He misses you. Next time, I expect you to be there."

"You got it," I say, but I'm unsure how convincing it sounds.

Winter spins around and links arms with Jeremy before I can gauge how much she believes my response. I think of us by the Viper Room a few weeks ago, a trail of peonies left for River Phoenix, scabs on my knees from crouching in the alleyway while I glugged from a bottle. I try to recall if I felt happy doing it. I know I was happy when I sang in front of the crowd at Freight Train and when the lights blacked out and Evan and I kissed for the first time outside in the rain. I wasn't high then, perfectly sober to fully remember the moment.

I watch Winter and Jeremy dancing away. She sings "Jeremy" to him in a loud cockney British accent and he whines for her to shut up. My two messes, messier than they ever seemed before. A chill buzzes down my spine as I wonder if their messiness might grow old, and I'll tire of cleaning up their spills.

The bell rings again, a final warning. I swivel around and book it back into the building. I'm not positive what class I have, since it'd been a millennia when I last showed up; but I'm pretty sure it might be pre-calc. The teacher would definitely be surprised when I arrive on time, whoever the crap mans the blackboard.

27

• • • • •

The Sign – Ace of Motherfucking Base

The rest of the semester passes pretty quickly. I realize if I actually show up to class it isn't that hard to get decent marks, and I'm able to bring up my grade point average to a pretty spectacular B-. Now I just have to wait for scholarships to start rolling in. Sarcasm. Yeah, so I'm kinda thinking about applying to college next year. Berklee doesn't look half bad if I keep bringing up my grades and doing a shit ton of extracurricular activities, except I likely couldn't handle Bostonians telling me to pahk their cahs so I'll likely stay out West.

I decide to split my time between Mom and Dad, so if one gets on my nerves, I'll pass over the baton to the other. Dad's squeeze Annette isn't half bad. She looks like a hen but is pretty chill. She smokes cigarettes out of long holders and has pornographic art all over her walls, of couples having artsy sex. It's kinda hot to be honest. She owns a French restaurant called Tartuffe, which is the name of some old French play. They serve really great coq au vin and sometimes

I'll do my homework at the bar while Annette has the chef fix me up a plate. She also never tries to be my mother because, at seventeen (that's right, I made it to seventeen!), I definitely don't need two.

Weirdo—excuse me—Mr. Ferguson and Mom have gotten even closer. Since they were neighbors they decided to build an extension between their houses. It's actually gonna be really cool once they finish, and he makes her happy, I guess, so who the hell am I to bitch and moan?

Once the summer begins, I get sick of both of the 'rents and decide to spend a week up in Ojai with Aunt Carly. She's gotten really into portraits and does a few of me that she plans to exhibit in a local gallery, so I'll have to come up again sometime for the opening. I can breathe well up there, away from L.A.'s chaos, knowing I've become as much of a country mouse as I'm a city one.

The other really dope thing I've been doing is taking voice and guitar lessons. It's from the same lady I went to when I was younger who totally remembered how talented I was. She's hardcore and won't let me screw around. Not a minute is wasted the three days a week that I go. I learn about pitch, rhythm, breathing, voice and diction, and my goal is to learn how to play a song on the guitar as well that Kristen would've enjoyed, although with my own grungy spin.

To pay for the lessons I got a job—yes, fuckers I can work too—I'm not just a blob. So I got a part-time gig at the CD store where Winter met that dude Vince. This guy named Mitch ran it and he has, like, a huge wealth of music knowledge. He has gray hair in a ponytail and always smells of weed, but he puts me onto some of the artists of his youth: Joplin who I knew about, but also CCR, Hendrix, The Doors, The Stones, and even The Beatles, who I find too Britishy sounding, but whose lyrics are super deep and meaningful.

Sometimes Winter comes by the CD store, but she wants to just mess around, and I actually have to work, so she stopped coming by as much. We still hang out, but between studying a crap ton so I won't flunk, flip-flopping between the 'rents places, a job and voice lessons, I don't have much spare time. I go over to her house and smoke a jay with her and Edina, but I feel like I'm doing charity work as opposed to it being natural. She still gets blasted out of her gourd with Jeremy and collected this new hanger-on called Emily, who I refer to as Emily Valentine from 90210, because she is Bad News Bears. Emily was hooking up with their dealer Raoul so there is mucho pot to spare all the time, and Winter partakes in this abundance with the kind of enthusiasm I'd never seen before. There are many times when I want to tell her to chill, but I keep my trap shut. Winter is even more stubborn than me, and she needs to hit her rock bottom on her own. Guiding her there would only make things worse. At least that's what I tell myself, so I won't feel like a terrible friend.

I write a letter to Stephen after getting the B- on my report card to show him how much better I'm doing. I thank him again for posting the bail in San Fran and for just being a cool guy. He writes back that he's been chosen by his Youth Organization to help build wells in Somalia because their water is so bad. Even though

I can't imagine what it'd be like to risk living in a place with bugs, famine and dysentery, he seems happy so I'm happy for him. He sends me a picture of him in a bright dashiki that he bought for the trip. I have to admit he looks like a tool in it, but a major sweet tool.

Evan and I actually stay in decent touch over the phone. Like when a boy says they'll call, you don't think they actually will. But Evan isn't a typical guy. He listens to my concerns about Winter and Jeremy and my excitement over my voice and guitar lessons. When Clarissa came back from Rome, the Grenade Bouquets got serious and booked a ton of shows. He's been writing a lot more too and wants to perform his own songs as opposed to just covers.

Around mid-July, he calls to say they'd booked a show in L.A. at this eighteen and over club.

"Will you be around, Nico?"

"Of course I'll be around!" I want to squeal but keep chill. It's been almost three months since we've seen each other. The only thing the two of us haven't discussed is if we're fooling around with anyone else. I'd had a few hookups, but mostly just making out and under-the-shirt stuff. I want to find out if he is seeing someone seriously, but I'm too afraid to ask.

"How's the guitar and singing lessons going?"

"Aces."

"You say you're learning one of your sister's favorite songs?"

"Yeah, I have it nailed. But it's, like, my own version of it. Not poppy at all. Super grungy of course."

"Why don't you play it at our show?"

"Really?"

"Yeah, we have a show in Vegas two days after so it's just a quick trip to L.A. But I'd love to see you and play music with you."

I wrap the phone cord around my finger until it cuts off the circulation.

"I'd love to play with you, too."

"So, what's the song?"

I tell him and he laughs hard. Evan has this great laugh, like his whole guts are erupting.

"The Bouquets'll help you do it justice," he says, and I want to say something powerful and meaningful, like, I love you, but all I say is, "looking forward to it."

• • •

I invite everyone important in my life to the Bouquets' show. My parents show up with their respective lovers: Annette looking hip and comfortable in a club and sucking on her cigarette holder, and Roger Ferguson coming off like he'd been dressed by a blind man, his shirt lopsided and half tucked in his too-tight pants, his comb-over not combed over nearly enough. But he stands there with his hand on my mom's back as she bops in place to the music playing over the speakers, "Plowed" by Sponge.

Dad drinks G and T's and makes small talk with Mom and Ferguson who owns a septic tank business. Yum. Mom and Dad try to outdo each other a little by boasting about their partners, and I like that they're keeping things feisty between them.

"Are you nervous?" Mom asks, playing with my hair because she obviously doesn't like what I'd done with it. "So blue," she says, fingering the ends.

Yeah, I've dyed my hair aqua blue. I don't love it, but it's growing on me a little.

"A little nervous," I say, chewing on a sleeve that's already sopping wet.

"Roger brought a video recorder to capture it. We can show all our friends!"

She's excited so I'll let that remark slide.

"I'm very proud of you in these last few months, Nico. You've really got your act together."

I wave away her adulation like it's no big deal.

"I love you, baby." She goes in for a kiss but I tell her no, since I don't want my make-up smeared. Besides, I spy Aunt Carly at the door and dance over.

"You made it!" I say, as we hug and I get tangled up in her crystals.

"Wouldn't miss it for the world," Carly says, her smile fading as she sees my dad.

"Come," I say, taking her by the hand and dragging her over to Dad.

"Peter," she says, tight-lipped.

"Carly," he says, even more tight-lipped.

"You both are ridiculous," I say, and push them together to give a forced hug. "Look, Kristen and I were way different, just like you guys, but…"

I stop and swallow, my breath stilted. I know I'll be dealing with Kristen today, but hadn't expected her name to come out of my mouth so casually.

"Like, you'll regret not making up with each other if anything ever happened," I say.

"She's right, Peter," Carly says, caressing one of her crystals for comfort.

Dad looks at me like he's pissed and proud at the same time.

"Can I buy you a drink, Carly?" he asks, indicating the bar. He neither smiles nor frowns, expressionless as ever, but at least that's a start.

I leave them all because Winter enters with Jeremy and my replacement—Emily, who's as skinny as a ladies cigarette and seems extra tortured with her ripped clothes and unwashed hair like straw.

"This place didn't even card me!" Jeremy says, after a hug. He's frosted his hair even more and started wearing make-up.

"It's eighteen and over," Emily sneers, as if nothing could be less cool. "I'm used to a twenty-one and over club."

"So, there's the door if you want to go to one," I say, fake-smiling.

Jeremy laughs at my retort, but Winter doesn't.

"What time are you going on?" Winter asks, eyes glassy.

"Probably at the end of their set. Why?"

"Just this party later we're gonna hit up," she says, with an affected yawn.

"Don't let me keep you."

"Emily, get me a double vodka soda," Winter says, pushing the girl toward the bar. "You know I'm good for it."

Emily listens like a trained geisha and leaves to get her master a drink.

"Wrapped around your finger much?" I ask.

"Nothing wrong with being a loyal friend," Winter replies.

"Ladies, ladies," Jeremy says, rubbing his temples. "Can we save World War Tres for another time?"

"I don't want a war," I say, staring down at the untied laces on my Doc Martens.

"Sure you do," Winter says, licking her teeth that look like the enamel had been scraped off from sucking on too many lemons. Then she cackles. "I'm just kidding, Nico. Where's your sense of humor?"

"It never went away," I say.

"Can you promise me that?"

Emily returns with Winter's drink that she sucks down like it's water. I'm about to tell her to slow down, but the words stay trapped in my throat. She looks at me desperately, like she's been begging for me to say something.

I feel someone's palms wrap around my eyes and turn around to see Lacey.

"Nico!"

We hug and I introduce her to Winter and Jeremy, not bothering with Emily. Ed, Randy, and Clarissa come over too. They have twelve shows booked after this one, on tour for the next three weeks.

"Looks like we'll finally get out of the red," Lacey says. "At least for a minute."

Ed belches. "Sorry," he says. "Just helps me get out the nerves for a set."

"You look great, Nico," Clarissa says. "Loving the blue."

You better not be doing Evan, I think, but I smile and complement the strappy dress she wears over a T-shirt.

We each tell each other good luck and she leaves

with Ed and Randy to grab a quick drink before they go on.

"So the Bouquets' are really doing well?" I say to Lacey.

"Yeah, I mean there will always be problems. Randy still sweats Evan, and Clarissa still sweats him as well."

"Oh, so Evan doesn't sweat her?" I casually ask.

"Calm down that puss, Nico," Winter says, and she and Jeremy guffaw.

"Evan has really just been focusing on the band," Lacey says. "No girls."

"I've been the same, like, focusing on my voice and guitar lessons."

"No girls either?" Lacey winks.

"Yeah, strictly dicky, Lacey, sorry."

"Girl's gotta try."

"I love the grandma glasses," Jeremy says to her. "Where do you get your fashion ideas?"

"I like mixing eras up," Lacey says.

"Hella cool," Jeremy replies. "I feel like the nineties are becoming so over. I wanna fish out my Dad's old bell-bottoms and rock them."

"I know this great vintage store on Melrose."

"Oh girl, do tell," he says, latching onto her hand. "Lemme buy you a drink."

When they leave, I cut Emily with my eyes so she'll get the hint and peace the hell out too. Winter finally gestures for her to jet and she saunters away.

"So, where's this boy you've been gushing over?" Winter asks.

"I haven't seen him yet."

"Good luck on stage tonight," she says, grinding

her teeth. "Seriously. I mean, I really can't wait to hear you."

We sway to the song "Molly" by Sponge and pucker our lips at the same time, sealing our roller-coaster friendship with a kiss.

Over her shoulder, I spy Evan's wavy blond hair, which he'd let grow. It goes down to his shoulders now. When he sees me, he immediately smiles and tucks a lock behind his ear.

"That your prince?" Winter asks, nodding at him with her chin.

Evan picks up the pace as he rushes over. "Hey, Nico."

We go in for a hug and then an awkward kiss on each of our cheeks like we are Europeans.

"It's good to see you."

"You too."

Both of us are acting shy so we avoid eye contact. There are a lot of "ums" and "uhs" before smooth talker Winter jumps in.

"I'm her best friend Winter," she says, giving him a hard handshake.

"Oh cool," he says. "Yeah, I heard a lot about you. You told Nico to run away so I guess I should thank you or we never would have met."

"Yeah, I'm a regular goddamn Cupid."

Evan smiles because he doesn't know what to say next. "So...uhh...are you ready to hear your girl sing?"

"I'm pissing my pants in anticipation."

"Oh, haha."

"Winter, I would love a beer before I go on." I kick at my guitar case by her foot in case she doesn't catch the signal that I want to be alone with Evan.

"I'm sorry," Winter says, bowing. "I'm eternally blasted outta my brain and I twist my words up like a dictionary in a blender."

She pulls me close, her lips against my earlobe. "He has a nice tushy, Nico. Make sure you get some before he leaves town."

"Thanks, Wint."

She plays with my hair. I can't tell if her eyes are tearing or just glassy from whatever she'd consumed.

"My baby's growing up," she says, and then more softly, "maybe someday I will too."

"Winter..." I reply, reaching out to grab her and hold her close and tell her how wonderful and special she is even when she isn't high. But she pirouettes away toward the bar before I get the chance. More and more, I wonder if we'll act strange with one another, a divide clearly surfacing. I look out to find her by the bar but she's vanished, blocked by the crowd.

"Your friend is...funny," Evan says.

"Yeah, she's something, I guess."

"So the band really practiced the version of the song you gave us," he says. "I love the chord progressions, it changes it from super pop and sunny to full of sorrow, but like, hopeful too at the end."

"That's my story," I say.

"You look really great. Healthy."

"I am. Been eating my veggies. And I dig the hair."

"Yeah, I actually have to use a brush now." He flips his locks like a valley girl, and I laugh. "It's really good to see you, Nico."

"You too."

"Well, we're about to go on, but let's grab a bite after. We're leaving early in the morning, but you and me, this all-night taco place off Mulholland I know of...."

"Aces. I'll bring my hungry."

He kisses me on the cheek. His lips hover as if they want more. We'll see how the tacos go, but I imagine us kissing up on Hollywood Hills by the famous sign like we are in some teen movie.

"Okay. Good luck, Nico. You're gonna kill it up there."

I mime stabbing the air with a knife as he makes his way toward the stage. The rest of Grenade Bouquets follows him and launches into a delicious set with some covers, but mostly Evan's new songs he'd told me about. As I make my way to the front of the stage, I don't know if he's looking at me the whole time, but I imagine he is, just like everyone else probably does. His new songs are pretty and sad. One is about his brother Chris and how he finally visited the VA hospital in Boise after being afraid to see Chris in that kind of mental state and how it brought his family closer together once he did. The final song he sings is called "Runaway." I have a shiver in my bones when he says the title. It's about a wild girl (guilty) who finds herself after running away and the boy who falls for her along the trip. How they are two crazy souls who are a little less crazy when they fuse together. The chorus goes "two wrongs make a right, and we can be together when the timing is right." I nearly jizz in my leotard when he sings, even though he rhymes "right" with "right." He winks his alien blue eye at me when the song finishes, and I melt into a delicious puddle of ice cream.

"For our last number, we have something very special for you. The inspiration for the song 'Runaway'!" he cheers as the crowd woo-hoos along with him. "Ladies and motherfucking gentleman, we have Nico Sullivan who sung for us once in Portland and literally brought the house lights down. Nico, come on up here."

I don't know how I'm able to get my legs to move properly, but they manage to get me up on stage. Evan gestures at the microphone. "It's all yours, star."

"Thank you," I gush. I settle the guitar strap around my neck and face the audience. "I want to thank Grenade Bouquets for letting me play with them. This is a cover song I've been tooling around with for a while, and it's for someone who's not here anymore but would've really dug it." I inhale a large swallow of breath as I get my courage together. "This is for you, Kristen. Kelly to my Brenda. Love you."

I turn to Evan who gives me a thumbs up and launches into a thrashing and mournful rendition of "The Sign" by Ace of Base as if Nirvana takes over the reins. I strum along, my fingers feeling like they are getting cut up right from the jump, but I can't stop. I put my lips against the mic and chant directly to my sister. Clarissa sings back up, but Kristen the ghost forms in her place as we hit the chorus. I swallow tears, but Kristen shakes her head.

I understand that life can be demanding without understanding.

"No more tears, baby sis, not for me anymore," Kristen says. She seems more at peace than when her ghost had visited me before. "I've accepted what's happened to me, it's time for you to do the same. You can remember me all you want and I'll always be there when you want to conjure me back. But promise me no more tears because I'm no longer crying either. I'll be happy just watching you bloom from above."

I'll take Kristen on tour with me, in whatever band I eventually wind up joining through the years because this is what I'm fucking meant to do with my life, through small cities and minuscule venues to large arenas someday when I'll need her support the most to get my frightened ass up on stage.

I blink as Kristen turns back into Clarissa when we near the end of the song. I've accepted her death too, no longer enraged at her being yanked away from me too soon. Evan comes up behind, shouting the chorus into the microphone as well, holding me up because my voice is starting to waver.

But I'll never fucking quit.

A gust of wind swings the front door of the club open, and Kristen's ghost departs, the bob of her yellow head getting smaller and smaller until it's gone. But I don't need to empty any more tears. I'm at peace too. I look out into the sea of faces supporting me. Mom and Ferguson. Dad and Annette clapping along. Jeremy shaking his booty with Lacey. Winter ignoring hella whack Emily, her fingers folded together as if she's praying, mouthing the words of a song I know she hates more than any other.

I turn back toward Evan who joins me again at the microphone; his blue eyes locked on only me as we shout out the final verse and collapse in each other's arms.

A rush of cheers echoes off the walls when we finish. We are panting as he takes my face in his hands.

"Your sister would've really loved that."

"I know," I say, gulping down the words and letting them settle in my belly. "She was here singing along."

"She always will be."

He kisses me in front of the audience who whoops and hollers.

After everyone's massive congratulations, we leave and he drives me to that all-night Mexican place near Mulholland Drive he knows. We eat our tacos on the hood of his car as we watch the misty smog settle over L.A.

"Why don't you join us for our show in Vegas?" Evan says, a blob of guacamole on the side of his mouth. "We can have you as our closer with that sweet freakin' version of 'The Sign'. And for other dates too."

"Won't Clarissa get pissed?"

"Ace of Base has two female singers, why can't Grenade Bouquets?"

I hoover a final bite of taco.

"You have guac dripping down your chin," I say, and wipe it away.

"See I'm a mess and need you to take care of me," he says. "It'll just be for the rest of the summer. Not when school starts up again."

A breeze blows by with the faint hint of Sunflowers

perfume that Kristen used to wear.

A sign? I wonder. Pointing me in the right direction?

I look back toward the Hollywood Hills, the sound of a chugging train rattling in my eardrums.

I nod yes as the train stops, finally reaching its station.

28

• • • • •

BONUS TRACK

Ready to Guide - Nico

I'm at Kristen's grave, heading to Vegas tomorrow. Evan and the rest of Grenade Bouquets have already left on their flight for their show in two days. My parents both okayed me to spend the rest of summer break on tour, as long I promised I'd be back before school started up. They were both so impressed by my singing I think they finally understand it can be my future.

It's morning and the graveyard is empty. I've brought along a tape recorder. After parting with Evan once our taco date finished and we made sure to stay firmly at first base (there'd be more time for that later), I rushed home and a flow of lyrics poured out of my brain. I no longer wanted to write "Nico's Lament," since I feel exhilarated now as opposed to miserable. While the Bouquets only booked me to sing my version of "The Sign," I want to prove I'm a songwriter as well, and an ode to Kristen would be the perfect way to showcase my chops.

"Hey Kelly," I say, running my hand over Kristen's tombstone. "This is for you."

I push record, clear my throat, and open myself up.

Your ghost remains inside

Ready to guide
Your ghost remains inside
Ready to guide
The tears have turned to dust
A smile now is a must
Bucket list done
But many more adventures to come
Scars have healed
Wounds no longer appeal
You've brought out my voice
And I've made the right choice
This train doesn't need to run away
I'm on the right pathway
And when I'm feeling low
My Kelly specter can glow
Because your ghost remains inside
Ready to guide
Your ghost remains inside
Ready to guide
So it'll never be goodbye
Only till the next time
You'll stun them up in heaven
Like I know you will
God's lucky you have you
The afterlife now more fill
And when I'm old and done
And my time has come

We can reunite for real
But for now, sadness has no appeal
Because your ghost remains inside
Ready to guide
Your ghost remains inside
Ready to guide
Ready to guide
Ready to guide

I stop recording, eject the cassette tape, and rest it on top of Kristen's tombstone. I walk away, but I'll return after my tour ends once the leaves have turned, with the promise of a new song to sing to her, always.

Love, your Surly Fuckin' Brenda. Xoxo.

ACKNOWLEDGMENTS

There are many people to thank that helped bring Runaway Train and Nico to life. Thank you to Nat Kimber at The Rights Factory for believing so much in the story and that readers would want a book about the grungy 1990s. Thank you to Rachel Del Grosso for your amazing edits. I'm new to Young Adult writing and learned a lot about making the book appropriate for young readers. And for wanting a second book in the series too! Thank you to Lauren Bridges and Tracey Govender at Wise Wolf Books for all the work you've put into Runaway Train as well. Thank you to my early readers Kat Bedrosian and Dani Grammerstorf-French for your notes and support. And to Ali McDonald for that first time at Tanner Smith's where I pitched the idea and you gave me the support to write it. Thank you to everyone who commented on a '90s thread three years ago on Facebook. So many suggestions about Nico's outfits and makeup (which I would have no clue about) made it into the final version, along with which celebrities she'd have a crush on and the shows she would watch (specifically 90210), which became a huge part of the book. And a huge thank you to all the musicians whose work influenced the novel and became chapter headings. The book is a love letter to grunge music and would not have been able to be written without the music of Nirvana, Hole, Soul Asylum, Stone Temple Pilots, Mother Love Bone, The Smashing Pumpkins, Pearl Jam, Temple of the Dog, Soundgarden, Tori Amos, L7, Mazzy Star, Faith No More, Green Day, Bush, R.E.M., and yes, even Ace of Motherfucking Base. Thank you!

ABOUT THE AUTHOR

• • • • •

Lee Matthew Goldberg is the author of the novels THE ANCESTOR, THE MENTOR, THE DESIRE CARD, SLOW DOWN and ORANGE CITY. He has been published in multiple languages and nominated for the 2018 Prix du Polar. After graduating with an MFA from the New School, his writing has also appeared in The Millions, Vol. 1 Brooklyn, LitReactor, Monkeybicycle, Fiction Writers Review, Cagibi, Necessary Fiction, the anthology Dirty Boulevard, The Montreal Review, The Adirondack Review, The New Plains Review, Underwood Press and others.

He is the editor-in-chief and co-founder of Fringe, dedicated to publishing fiction that's outside-of-the-box. His pilots and screenplays have been finalists in Script Pipeline, Book Pipeline, Stage 32, We Screenplay, the New York Screenplay, Screencraft, and the Hollywood Screenplay contests. He is the co-curator of The Guerrilla Lit Reading Series and lives in New York City. RUNAWAY TRAIN and its sequel, GRENADE BOUQUETS are his first Young Adult novels from Wise Wolf Books in 2021.

CPSIA information can be obtained
at www.ICGtesting.com
Printed in the USA
LVHW041728080421
683894LV00023B/996

9 781953 944047